Praise for
Culture Brand

"In his book, *Culture Brand*, Dr. Jay Raines tackles an important leadership responsibility: developing a winning culture. For leaders who view building a successful culture as a daunting responsibility, *Culture Brand* is a must-read. This book is thoughtfully written with real-world examples and tools and techniques leaders can use right away to develop a culture that will continue to build dividends beyond the life of the organization's current leadership team."

—**John Gronski**, Major General, U.S. Army, retired

"Dr. Jay Raines's *Culture Brand* is a masterful guide to transforming a company's cultural ideology into a powerful, enduring brand. It clearly shows that even the best products or services are short-lived without great people aligned uniformly around a shared mission. That mission starts with its culture. I highly recommend this book to anyone seeking to build a sustainable culture that represents the very fabric of their organization and serves as a strong foundation for years to come."

—**Ricky Dickson**, CEO and President (retired), Blue Bell Creameries

"Remarkable cultures don't happen by accident. They are intentionally designed and consistently reinforced. *Culture Brand* teaches leaders how to translate mission and values into everyday behaviors that create results, strong teams, and character-driven leadership. Jay Raines provides a framework that makes culture both actionable and sustainable, and you will be encouraged in your organizational culture journey."

—**Dee Ann Turner**, vice president, Chick-fil-A (retired), bestselling author, *Bet on Talent*

"One of the many moments of genius that Raines gives us is right there in the title: *Brand*—normally the realm of soft drinks and logos—is a rich lens for thinking strategically about who we are together. With great storytelling, Raines is an engaging guide in this journey of activating mission while leaning into our beautiful humanity. Bravo!"

—**David Hutchens**, author, CEO of The Storytelling Leader

"Leaders know a healthy culture drives performance. Unfortunately, too few understand how to design one. That's about to change if you will read and apply Culture Brand. Jay Raines is a seasoned voice who has created a practical roadmap for you to build the culture of your dreams!"

—**Randy Gravitt**, CEO of Lead Every Day, author of *Winning Begins at Home*

"*Culture Brand* delivers a strategic framework that treats culture with the weight it deserves. Raines challenges the traditional path of promotion with a 'Ladder of Development' that balances hard skills with people skills, proving that winning cultures are led by design rather than default. If you are tired of mission drift and want to align your team from the C-suite to the front line, this is the blueprint you've been waiting for."

—**Bill Forster**, CEO and founder, CEO Zones

"*Culture Brand* is one of those rare leadership books that takes something leaders talk about loosely: culture. He turns it into something concrete, operational, and hard to ignore. Having known and learned from Jay Raines for years, I can say this book reflects how he actually coaches: clear, practical, and relentlessly focused on results without losing the human core. If you're a leader tired of slogans and ready to design culture instead of hoping for it, this is a serious, usable framework—not a feel-good read."

—**Bert Cherian**, CEO, Meta Results Pvt. Ltd. (India)

"Immensely readable and immediately applicable, *Culture Brand* is like EQ for organizations. Jay Raines leverages his breadth of experience to kindly, gently, but effectively help leaders lead through the lens of culture. The book is full of practical communication tools that move culture from simple words to everyday actions. Read *Culture Brand*, and you'll never see organizational culture the same way again."

—**Jeff Davenport**, principal, executive speaker
coach at Davenport Communications

"As Dr. Jay Raines expertly points out, great culture is the foundation of excellent organizations. Cultures that focus on genuine care for teammates, customers, and a relentless pursuit of excellence will have a distinct advantage in the marketplace."

—**Ryan Magnon**, COO, Ithaka Hospitality Partners

"*Culture Brand* was a wake-up call for me. I realized I had been practicing culture by default instead of intentionally designing it as a leader. This framework gave me the clarity and responsibility to own culture rather than hope it would take care of itself."

—**David Howell**, MS, PhD, president and
CEO at Bondwell Technologies

"Dr. Jay Raines has done an amazing job of providing guidance and direction on how to define and implement culture in his book *Culture Brand*. The book provides a framework for company leaders to follow in communicating strategies that can help propel their organization well into the future."

—**Todd Huckabee**, president and CEO, Crockett National Bank

"*Culture Brand* is a practical and powerful reminder that when leaders design culture with intention, alignment follows and results accelerate. Through relatable stories and clear frameworks, Jay Raines shows how culture becomes a measurable force that drives teamwork, accountability, and sustained performance."

—Kelly Sartain, CEO, Leadership Consultancy

"*Culture Brand* is a clear, actionable playbook for building a high-performance culture. Jay blends story and strategy in a way that moves leaders from insight to execution. You can immediately apply what you learn—whether in a leadership meeting or a strategic offsite. I wholeheartedly recommend both this book and deeply trust Jay's work."

—Lantz Howard, executive coach, founder and CEO, Lead Wholeheartedly

"What sets *Culture Brand* apart is its immediate applicability. Raines equips leaders to see themselves as Chief Culture Officers and gives them real-time tools to put values into action. The Calls to Action throughout the book are practical, thoughtful, and usable, making this book especially valuable for leaders who want to move from concept to practice without overcomplication. Coaches will also find it incredibly useful as a shared language and framework for guiding leaders through meaningful conversations about values, behavior, and results."

—Melissa Eisenbrandt, personal development and leadership coach, Royal Coaching Colorado

"*Culture Brand* is exactly what growing organizations need. Instead of hoping your culture just happens, Dr. Raines delivers an actionable system through real-world stories and examples, showing you how to design, document, and scale a culture that drives your mission—providing a culture guidebook for every team member, at every location."

—Edwina Adams, speaker, consultant, founder of Authentic Authority Academy

"Great culture grows great people, and great people grow great work. *Culture Brand* is the tool that will help you get the soil right so your team and business grow and thrive in all seasons. Jay has given you everything you need to grow something amazing. Don't just read it; put it into practice."

—**Brian Prue**, CEO of MissioGroup

"Our organization has directly benefited from these *Culture Brand* principles. If you are a leader struggling to find tangible ways to design the culture you need, this book will provide the roadmap for that journey."

—**Kevin Friar**, CEO, Hoover CS

"*Culture Brand* turns culture from an abstract concept into a practical operating system for leaders. Jay provides a clear framework for intentionally designing culture and aligning people, decisions, and systems around mission as organizations grow. This book is especially valuable for leaders who want culture to scale with clarity rather than drift with complexity."

—**Daniel Higbee**, CEO at OneClickApp.com

"Dr. Raines hits the nail on the head with regard to the importance of culture. I wish I would have had a reference point like this back in 2013, when we started our company. Thank you, Jay, for gifting us with your insight!"

—**Michael Perkins**, owner, Inspire Physical Therapy

"Great cultures are built when people feel connected to a shared mission and when leaders model the behavior they want to see in their teams. Jay has an incredible gift for helping organizations ask the questions that align people, clarify vision, and bring teams along in a meaningful way. *Culture Brand* captures this truth practically and serves as a powerful guide for leaders who want to live the culture they're building, not just talk about it."

—**Jordan Annis**, founder, reShift app

"*Culture Brand* is an actionable and inspiring guidebook for leaders who want to build culture by design rather than by default. Packed with pro tips, clear frameworks, and practical calls to action, it serves as an evergreen tool for shaping, scaling, and sustaining intentional workplace culture. CEOs, executive teams, and culture champions will find it especially valuable as they move from managing operations to embodying the role of Chief Culture Officer."

—**Charles Hooper, Jr.**, MCC, executive coach
and leadership development advisor
hoopercoaching.com

"*Culture Brand* cuts through the noise! Jay helps leaders unpack the vital leadership qualities of character, teaming, and results. *Culture Brand* helped us align around our organization's DNA to bring clarity and accelerate momentum for business. Our young leaders are more effective and are engaged in the activity of multiplying the qualities that deliver growth in all facets of our enterprise."

—**Bruce Ploeser**, multi-location owner-operator,
Chick-fil-A Goodyear and Chick-fil-A Estrella, Goodyear, Arizona

"Dr. Raines puts together decades of experience, a library's worth of education, and an educator's heart to make this a great, concise guide to culture building and team alignment. It's a must-read!"

—**TK Douglass**, CEO and owner, Fidelis Creative Agency

"*Culture Brand* offers a powerful yet simple framework for aligning people, purpose, and performance. As a business owner, I appreciate how practical and scalable this approach is for protecting culture while growing an organization. This book equips leaders with the tools needed to ensure their mission is lived out daily, not just something written on the wall."

—**Jarell Carter**, founder and CEO, Momentum Fitness

"I would give this book 5 out of 5 stars because it's practical. It takes what you're reading and helps you do something with it! I promise you will walk away healthier, more focused, and most of all, more aligned with truly what matters most."

—**Charlie Rhea**, EOS implementer and business coach, EOS Worldwide

"Many of the concepts in *Culture Brand* resonate directly with real challenges our organization faces. Rather than treating culture as a buzzword, Dr. Jay Raines offers a clear, practical framework that makes culture something leaders can intentionally design, measure, and scale as their organizations grow."

—**Jay Maxwell**, CEO, The Arena Group

"I have always admired how Jay has integrated his global cross-cultural leadership with what he has learned and taught. The payoff for his valuable experience is found in his new book, *Culture Brand*. Each chapter of the book provides clear and actionable steps to move your leaders from accidental, reactive leadership to intentional culture design that can build your organization to be more profitable but also be a meaningful, motivating place to work for your stakeholders."

—**Michael J. Griffin**, CEO Equipping Leaders for Asia Pte. Ltd. (Singapore)

"No hype or hyperbole; the concepts and framework for building and sustaining intentional culture from Jay Raines in his new book are truly powerful and capable of transforming organizations.
"I have witnessed this firsthand in my own organization and have seen myriad examples in others. *Do not* sleep on this book. If you are a leader, your team deserves it!"

—**Ryan Twitchel**, executive director of development,
Chick-fil-A locations in Tempe, Arizona

"With *Culture Brand,* Jay takes a concept that most see as an abstract hope and shows how it can be a designed future. I highly recommend this book for anyone looking to develop their team and improve their business results."

—**Jon Morris**, operator, Chick-fil-A Golf Mill, Niles, Illinois

"As a mama of six, entrepreneur, and founder, I don't have time for leadership books that just sound nice but don't actually help.

"*Culture Brand* isn't that.

"This book doesn't just inspire. It equips. From the moment I read 'never blame the crop,' I knew I was holding something special. It reminded me that it's not about fixing people. It's about tending the soil and creating environments where people can actually thrive.

"That's leadership. That's culture.

"Whether you're leading a company or a dinner table (or both at once, as I often am), this book will serve you well."

—**Dani Goeppert**, cofounder, Scale with Stability Summit

"*Culture Brand* is destined to do for team culture what *The Goal* did for operations management. This book is offers actionable business fable and relevant anecdotes to provide an easily usable road map to improve business results in any setting."

—**Wayne Wisniewski**, president, Tala Energy

CULTURE BRAND

A Proven Framework for
Building a Culture That Wins

JAY RAINES

Culture Brand

© 2026 by Jay Raines

This book is available at special discounts when purchased in quantity for use as premiums, promotions, fundraisers, or for educational purposes. For inquiries and details, contact the author at culturebrandbook@leadersq.com.

LeadersQ Publishing
Bryan, Texas
LeadersQ.com

Cover Design by Amy McMurry
Editing and Interior Design by My Writers' Connection

Library of Congress Control Number: 2026902630
Hardback: 978-1-950714-57-5
Paperback: 978-1-950714-58-2
eBook: 978-1-950714-59-9

First Printing: February 2026

LEADERSQ

In memory of my friend
and mentor, Scott Clark.

CONTENTS

How did I get here?

Kate sank into the comfortable armchair and sighed. Damp and slightly chilled from the sudden downpour, she had escaped into a cozy coffee shop. It had been a long day—a string of long days.

The man who had welcomed her moved with calm purpose, first ushering her to the armchair, then quickly clearing a nearby table. A hum of conversation mixed with the soft clinking of coffee cups being sorted behind the bar to create a reassuring clatter of care. The ambiance was one of order amidst chaos, with a busy but unrushed rhythm.

And it didn't hurt that the delightful aromas of coffee and freshly baked pastries filled the air.

Kate needed this—not just the chair but also a moment of calm and a warm, welcoming place to relax. Lately, the office had been the last place she felt welcome. She was the boss—and yet sometimes, she felt like she didn't belong there at all.

She looked out the window, searching for signs of the midday sun. Instead, she saw fat drops of rain pelting pavement, passersby scurrying to find shelter, an umbrella salesman setting up to make quick, easy money. Her gaze softened as she watched the rain trace paths down the windowpanes. The sounds of the busy shop faded as her thoughts turned inward.

Culture Brand

Exhaustion overwhelmed her. *How did I get here?* Kate rested her head against the soft chair and closed her eyes.

She had jumped at the opportunity to lead Intelex a year ago. The CEO position seemed like a dream—at first. The large tech company had all the right components: a great product, an all-star leadership team, and market readiness. Intelex had experienced early success, and she knew that if she could get the business streamlined, there was huge potential for growth.

During the past several months, however, it had become clear that things just weren't working. The company had not been able to move the needle. Worse than sales and revenue being stagnant, it seemed as if the different departments were actually working against one another.

And now it seemed her executive team was working against her. Earlier that day, she learned that at least two of her VPs were questioning her leadership—not to her face, of course, but the gossip was unsettling.

What had started as her dream job was turning into a nightmare. If she didn't get the organization moving in sync and in the right direction—and soon—she feared she would lose everything she'd worked for.

"Your latte is ready."

Kate opened her eyes to see the man setting the small cup on the table next to her.

She smiled. "Thank you."

Just as he turned to leave, Kate stopped him. "Sir, I was impressed with the young lady who took my order. She seems to love her job." She picked up the small porcelain cup and took a sip of the rich espresso drink. "For that matter, so do you."

"I do. And yes, that's Maria. She's amazing," he said, casting a quick glance at the woman at the register. "I can't imagine not having her on my team. In fact, I wouldn't be surprised if she ends up running this place one day."

How did I get here?

"Your team? Are you one of the managers?"

"You could say that," he said with a proud smile. "I'm Scott Drake. This is my shop."

Kate felt the heat of embarrassment on her face. "I'm sorry." She shook her head and started over. "I mean, it's a lovely place. It's just a little surprising to see the owner bussing tables. Especially when you have such great employees."

The Coffee Nook had excellent reviews and was frequently recognized for its quality and service. These days, it seemed as if there were a coffee shop on every block in the downtown area—and not all of them survived. But this place had a solid reputation and was clearly thriving despite the fierce competition.

Scott's kind smile put her at ease. "I'm glad we were able to serve you. The truth is, my team doesn't need me to bus tables—or do much of anything else—but I enjoy helping out now and then. It keeps me in touch with what's going on, not just on paper but in real life."

He moved to wipe down a nearby table. He pushed in the chairs, then paused and took in the scene: customers enjoying their food and drinks, team members working on task to keep things running smoothly. He smiled again and said, "Our team may look polished now, but you might be surprised at how far we've come. A few years ago, I wasn't sure we were going to make it."

Her interest piqued, she said, "That's a story I'd like to hear." And she meant it. At a loss for how to turn Intelex around, Kate was desperate for ideas—or at least a little hope. She was open to wisdom, wherever the source—even if it came from the owner of a quaint coffee shop.

Scott smiled thoughtfully. He flagged down a nearby worker and asked for a cup of coffee, then took a seat in the armchair across from her. "Let's see," he said. "Where should I start?"

An hour later, Kate had taken pages of notes in her journal and a heart full of hope. Scott's inspiring story was exactly what she needed to hear, and she had a few ideas for her next steps with her team.

The afternoon traffic on the drive home gave her plenty of time to think about what was working and what wasn't. She felt confident, for instance, about all the work her team had done to define their purpose, values, vision, and mission during their most recent off-site meeting. The business's priorities were clear.

During their conversation, she mentioned to Scott that she was frustrated by the lack of progress, despite the fact that her team knew where the company was going and why their goals mattered.

His response surprised her: "The thing is, even with all the best plans and strategies, if your team isn't working together, nothing works. I had everything lined out on paper, but we're working with humans, not robots. Hearts, souls, minds . . . and all sorts of personalities. You've got to have something that brings everyone together. For my team, what it boiled down to was culture. Once we got the culture right, things changed. Bottom line? Culture gets results. Without it, even the best strategies fail."

Scott's coffee shop turnaround affirmed that even with those vital elements of purpose, mission, vision, and values identified, her team would fail if they didn't start working together.

Each of her VPs had been approaching challenges in their own ways. Truth be told, even she had her own way of doing things. The end result was that the leaders' personalities drove the way each team operated. And much of the time, those competing personalities clashed, both within and between departments. The result was mixed messages that repeatedly led to confusion, conflict, or unhealthy competition rather than collaboration.

After hearing Scott's story, she felt certain that with a unified approach—the how of working together—she had a shot at turning things around.

Culture Gets Results

Culture is not squishy. It is strategic.
—Jon Bridges, Chief Marketing Officer, Chick-fil-A

Two prevailing perspectives dominate conversations about organizational culture:

- **Culture doesn't really matter.** Leaders who hold this view doubt the practical value of culture. They don't see the point of trying to build or influence culture. To leaders with this perspective, shaping organizational culture feels a bit like scooping up air with their hands. They don't doubt that culture exists, but they believe it is intangible and difficult to measure. To these leaders, it seems more productive to focus on things they know they can control and calculate.

- **Culture does matter, but it's difficult to control.** Leaders with this belief know organizational culture is incredibly valuable, but it seems so big and nuanced that it is difficult to define, design, and manage. Focusing on one aspect of their organization's culture brings up questions and challenges about other areas. As soon as one challenge is tackled, three more arise. Culture seems like something that can't be controlled.

Whatever your current understanding or beliefs about culture, as you read this book, you'll discover that it is possible to design and create a healthy organizational culture—what our team calls *Culture Brand*. When you implement the Culture Brand framework, you'll see firsthand how the intentional work of designing, aligning, and scaling culture in your organization equips your team to stay on mission and work together, even when you—the team lead, manager, executive, or owner/CEO—aren't in the room.

For more than a decade, I have studied the concept of culture, exploring questions such as,

What is culture?

How important is it?

How do we measure and guide it?

How can we design and cultivate it into something incredible that helps our organizations win?

What I've learned, and what our coaches at LeadersQ have seen in action with our clients, is that **culture *does* matter, and we can design it with intention and purpose**. When we design culture well, it becomes the power that energizes an organization's mission, vision, and success.

Culture matters because culture gets results.

What Is Culture?

Culture is a word that we hear often in the business world, but like most words, it means different things to different people.

Let's look at a few ways we can harness the power of organizational culture.

Culture Drives Mission

You have probably heard the phrase "culture eats strategy for breakfast." While there is some debate about who coined this phrase, it resonates with leaders who have experienced resistance from their teams. Resistance to strategic change is frustrating and can bring progress to a halt. The best-laid plans are derailed by an unhealthy culture that refuses to change. This truth about the power of culture has an upside: a healthy culture is responsive and receptive. It fosters behaviors that promote growth, making it possible for good strategies to get *great* results. But there's more to culture than eliminating opposition.

Think of culture as an ocean wave headed for shore. Waves are relentless in reaching their destination. They push ahead, moving around and over opposition. Waves seem unstoppable. Organizational culture is the collective interplay of attitudes, behaviors, personalities, values, and relationships. In this way, culture can function like a personality with fairly predictable responses to its environment, and as leaders, our task is to harness the momentum and relentless force of culture to drive the organization's mission and strategic efforts.

Culture Aligns Individual Effort to the Team Mission

When you find a way to align culture with your mission, very little can stand in your way. The immense energy generated by people who are unified by culture and united in their mission can create an unstoppable force when directed at a clear vision.

Notice the words *align* and *unified*. When we're talking about mission, culture matters because it brings purpose to every task, outcome, and person within an organization. Let's use another analogy for aligning mission and culture. Imagine that your mission is a long rowboat, the kind used for racing in the Olympics. Your team members are the crew at the oars. The boat is aimed at the finish line: your vision.

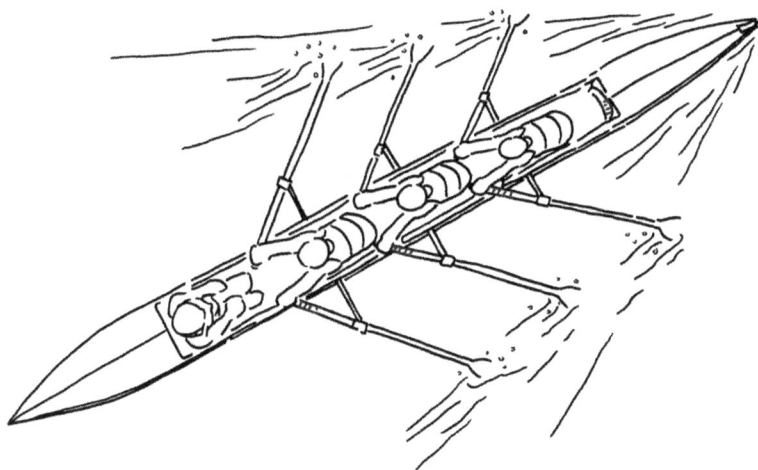

As the race begins, you notice several team members are off-beat, which slows the boat's progress. Other team members aren't just out of sync; they are rowing in the wrong direction! They're actually working against everyone else's efforts. If things keep going like that, you'll never win the race; you might not even reach the finish line. To compete and win, you've got to get everyone rowing in unison and in the right direction. You need everyone aligned—in mission, purpose, and effort—and aimed at the vision.

The same sort of scenario plays out in organizations every day. We all have team members who put so much effort into relationships that they don't quite get their tasks done. Then there are those who are so focused on the job that they look past or run over their coworkers. You might have another person on the team who is so confident in what they are doing that they are unwilling to receive feedback on what they're doing wrong.

This misaligned effort makes the work more frustrating. Everyone is working hard (too hard) with less reward for their efforts. A clear and measurable culture offers the solution to alignment and keeps the mission from drifting off course. When each person on the team can objectively evaluate whether their efforts are in alignment with the team's mission, people can work more efficiently and effectively *together*.

Culture Eliminates Friction

If I were to ask you right now what you wish would disappear from your organization, it is very likely that you would list behavioral problems related to friction. Disengagement, lack of ownership, inattention to goals, unkind treatment of others, a lack of sharing or development, and mistrust all create friction within organizations.

Friction typically arises from one of the two extremes of unhealthy cultures. Unhealthy cultures are either micromanaged or develop microcultures. Microcultures create factions within organizations that work against one another. Rather than creating a sense of community, these ununified microcultures can make people feel like they're living and working in the Wild, Wild West.

On the opposite end of the spectrum, micromanaged cultures are over-controlled. Fear and distrust are high.

In both instances, engagement is low, and innovation and efficiency are stifled. Unhealthy culture is filled with needless friction that costs time, energy, and resources.

Think of that rowboat again. If just one person holds their oars at the wrong angle or puts them in the water but refuses to row, they increase the friction—the resistance—and slow the whole team's progress. Eliminating friction gets results. Healthy cultures encourage unity, ownership, and communication, which accelerate trust, productivity, and innovation.

Culture Creates Synergy

Let's do something great! The most challenging part of that sentence is the word you don't see: *us. Us* means everyone must work together, and *us* is where synergy begins. The environment created by a healthy culture that drives mission, aligns your team members' efforts, and eliminates friction is one where synergy thrives.

So what is synergy? It's powerful! Synergy is when one plus one equals something greater than two. It's the effect that multiplies your team members' efforts and maximizes the power of inspiration. As an example, let's say you have one team member who is great at 90 percent of their role. In a healthy culture, when another team member comes alongside that person with their unique skillset, the result of their combined effort isn't simply 100 percent or even 180 or 200 percent. The fascinating and magical math of synergy is that we get more done together than we could ever do individually. This phenomenal force cannot survive in an unhealthy culture where divided and often divisive microcultures stifle progress.

Greatness may start with inspiration, but it isn't enough to complete that objective. Teams need the challenge and momentum that come from working with people who are focused on the same goal. When that goal is "something great"—something beyond what any one person can do alone— teams need the X-factor of synergy.

Call to Action

Each chapter will have a call to action to help you apply the steps one at a time. The call to action for this introduction is to reflect on these two questions:

1. What are the costs of *not* having a healthy culture in your team or organization?

2. Name three current behavior or attitude "frictions" in your team or organization right now.

PART ONE:
BE A CULTURE LEADER

The *how* is culture, and it's what we're missing.

For the first time in months, Kate felt excited about being in the office. She smiled as she unlocked her office door. Things were going to be different. The members of her leadership team were all professionals. They wanted to succeed as much as she did. Surely, they would be just as eager as she was to create a sense of unity within the culture of the organization.

Kate dropped her leather tote on her desk. Ideas had been buzzing in her mind all morning. Still smiling, she powered up her computer. While she waited for it to come to life, a message flashed on her phone's screen. Tapping it, she saw it was a new calendar appointment.

12:00–2:00 p.m. Bill Sanders.

Her smile faded, as did the enthusiasm she'd felt only seconds before. It seemed as if the oxygen had been sucked out of the room, leaving the air thick with worry. Taking a steadying breath to clear her mind, she rolled her shoulders to work out the sudden tension.

Bill was a mentor, a friend even, but he was also on her company's board. She knew from experience that an impromptu meeting with a board member was rarely a good thing. In light of the rumors she'd heard the day before about a few of her VPs talking behind her back, her hopes weren't high that this was simply a friendly visit.

Kate tapped ACCEPT on the calendar invitation and sent her assistant a message to have lunch for two delivered to her office for their meeting.

She still had a few hours to formulate her plans for what she'd begun to think of as a culture transformation. The more she thought about it, the more certain she was that Scott's leadership journey at The Coffee Nook provided a path to the kinds of changes she and her team needed to make. Those changes centered on creating a healthy company culture—one that was unified and would enable them to move forward together. Sure, Intelex was many times larger than the little coffee shop, but she couldn't see any reason the principles wouldn't apply. Would her executives be open to the ideas? Would they listen, or had they given up on her as a leader? Those concerns circled in her mind for a moment.

Kate picked up her phone and dialed the number for The Coffee Nook. Recognizing Scott's voice on the other end of the line, she offered a quick greeting, then said, "I know we're both busy, so I'll get to the point. I've been thinking about what you shared with me yesterday, and I would really like my team to hear your story. What does your schedule look like next week?"

By the time she disconnected the call, Kate was smiling to herself again. Scott had agreed to come to next week's leadership meeting. Kate pulled the journal from her tote and began to transfer her notes to a planning document. The culture at Intelex needed to change— and she believed that if her team could figure out how to work and win together, they would be unstoppable.

As her fingers flew across the keyboard, her thoughts wavered back and forth between hope and worry. Would the methods that had worked for his small coffee shop apply to her multimillion- dollar organization? She was willing to find out.

She just hoped it wasn't too late.

Bill Sanders showed up right at noon, and their lunch arrived a few minutes later. They ate at the small table near the window in her office. The view from fifty stories up on this remarkably clear day overlooked the city's chrome-and-glass buildings and rooftop gardens.

It didn't take long for Bill to get to the point of their meeting. Taking a break between bites, he said, "Kate, you know how much I respect you. I recognized your drive for results and your leadership potential when we worked together years ago. So when Intelex needed a new CEO, I was happy to recommend you to the board."

"Thank you, Bill. I am grateful for your faith in me."

"Of course, of course." Bill nodded. Leaning back a bit, he folded his hands and studied her for a moment.

"The thing is, Kate, the board is beginning to question whether they made the right choice. You've been here a year, and, for some reason, this team is not pulling together as we had hoped. The board doesn't know you like I do, and they are concerned about your ability to turn this team around."

Kate took a sip of water as she considered how to respond, but Bill continued. "Also, as a friend, I thought I should tell you that more than one of your leaders has mentioned concerns about a lack of confidence in your leadership."

Appalled, Kate readied to defend herself. Gossip was one thing, but going to a board member with a complaint was out of line. Bill recognized the shock in her expression and waved a hand as if to brush off her concern. "No, no. Not formal complaints, Kate." He reached for his fork and loaded it with a bite. "Just country club chatter. You know how it is."

She did. Gossip and complaints were the norm for a few of her executives. She smoothed the napkin in her lap and took a beat to let her blood pressure settle. It wasn't all that surprising to learn she'd been a topic of discussion on the golf course.

"I understand. I am disappointed also." *More than you know*, she thought. Kate folded her napkin and laid it on the table beside her mostly untouched plate. Looking across the table at her mentor, she chose her words carefully. "We have taken all of the conventional steps to set our course. You've seen our business plan, and the board seemed enthusiastic about our vision and priorities."

"Yes, it's a solid plan." Bill nodded and shifted in his chair. "That's what makes this challenging. The other board members are doubtful you will be able to reach those goals."

"I was too. Until yesterday."

Creases lined the man's forehead as he raised his eyebrows in curiosity. "I'm all ears," he said, prompting her to continue.

"For a while now, I've had this sense that something is missing. We have several key elements in place. What we don't have is unity. Our departments are working hard, but they don't always work *together*.

"We've done a great job identifying what's important to Intelex," Kate said. "Unfortunately, concepts are inherently difficult to measure. Our mission and vision statements are strong. And our values look great on the walls down there in the lobby. But we need a way for our executives and their teams to make concepts actionable and measurable. I met a business owner yesterday who told me how he had turned things around with his team by unifying them with a strong, healthy culture. I think we need to do the same thing. Our teams need to understand how Intelex's mission, vision, and values influence—or at least *should* influence—each person's behavior. The *how* is culture, and it's what we're missing."

The *how* is culture, and it's what we're missing.

Kate felt her confidence build as she spoke, convinced she was onto something. "When we get the culture right, I believe we'll be able to create the alignment we need between departments, and I know we'll gain momentum toward our goals."

Bill had listened quietly, but Kate could see the look of skepticism on his face. She took a sip of water and waited for his reaction.

"Honestly, Kate, it sounds a little too good to be true—too simple to be effective. Culture is a buzzword these days. You don't have time to waste chasing feel-good ideas when real-life results are what you need." He paused, then shrugged. "If you want to give it a shot—"

"I do," Kate cut in, sounding far more confident than she felt. "We've got a good team here, Bill. And a great product. I really believe the right culture will help us hit our targets."

CHAPTER 1

Culture Brand

*If you do not change direction, you may
end up where you are heading.*

—Lao Tzu

Culture, like community, forms when people speak the same language and share similar values. Shared language and values influence a group's behavior. There's a common understanding of what's important and the sense that *we're all in this together.* One of the challenges of coming into a new community is learning the social norms and societal rules. It's especially challenging because, although these *rules* are generally accepted, they are unwritten. If you don't know them or don't follow them, you'll never fit in. There will always be some distance or uneasiness between you and your neighbors.

My family lived in India for several years. To fit in to the community, we had to learn many new cultural habits—and unlearn a few old ones. To touch someone with your left hand or hand someone money or a business card using your left hand, for example, is socially unacceptable. The left hand is considered taboo, and touching someone or giving (or receiving) any item with your left hand is viewed as an insult.

It took time for me to get into the habit of only using my right hand when offering my business card or cash payment. Even after years of living in the West, where using one's left hand isn't an issue, I tend to reach awkwardly with my right hand when I'm handing my credit card through the driver's side window at the drive-thru. It's a habit.

It can take years to learn a culture's rules. I remember thinking, *Wouldn't it be nice if someone could give me a culture guidebook?* Having all the rules and customs written down in one place could have saved me countless embarrassing encounters. More than that, it would have improved the interactions I had with others right from the start. I could have fit in more quickly.

Culture shock doesn't just occur when people visit a different country. It also happens each time someone new joins your organization. That's because every team has a different culture. This book equips you to create that kind of culture guidebook, not for living or working abroad but to help everyone work more effectively within your organization. We'll look at the rules of culture engagement, what it takes to win together, and how to design your organization's culture so you can foster that critical sense of community that drives mission and creates momentum. At LeadersQ, we call this tool *Culture Brand*, and it is simple enough to be written on a napkin.

What Is Culture Brand?

Culture Brand is a customizable framework that sets the expectations for behavior for everyone at every level of your organization. It unifies your team members around your mission and vision so that *together* you can move faster, farther, and with more focus than ever before.

The next three sections of this book reveal how you can use this framework to lead people well by *designing* your organization's unique culture. You'll then discover how Culture Brand *aligns* people at every level—from new hires to seasoned executives—to the shared mission and vision. With that unified and focused effort, you'll be able to *scale* success.

Design ⟶ Align ⟶ Scale

Culture Brand

A Culture Brand is built from three basic aspects of team member behavior: results, teaming, and character. It's the combination of these three critical elements that yields success. To that end, your Culture Brand gives you and everyone on your team a common language to describe your organization's culture in just three words. Compared to the paragraph-long mission and vision statements you might be more accustomed to, three words may not sound like much. Trust me. What we've seen with our clients is that this powerful three-word approach to culture makes it clear and easy to remember and, at the same time, deep enough to provide a robust way to measure or track everything that is necessary for team members to succeed. A Culture Brand does not replace your organizational purpose or mission, but it guides everyone toward mission-driven behavior.

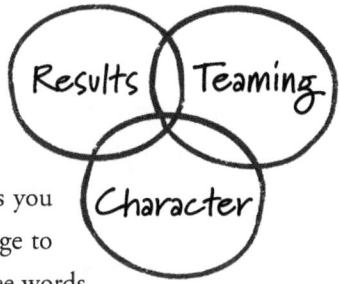

Your Culture Brand sets the expectation for how you will work together. It defines success and outlines how you want to represent the organization to your clients, vendors, and community. This three-word culture "guidebook" helps you and your team members stay focused on the mission. It also ensures that no one personality is responsible for driving or capable of derailing that mission. That may sound like a big promise, but that's why culture matters. It's *powerful*.

Let's look at a few of these elements of culture a little more closely.

A Common Language

Language is a key mark of a culture, which is why the first step to designing your Culture Brand is to discover the words that inspire your team to work together toward a shared mission and vision.

A single word can communicate volumes, but the same word can also mean different things to different people. The word *grit*, for example, used to remind me of sand in my turkey sandwich at the beach. Today, however, that same word is used in the business and sports worlds to exemplify the traits of tenacity, fortitude, and toughness. All that powerful meaning is wrapped up in one tiny word.

Your Culture Brand will help you harness the power of a common language. You'll discover how just a few meaning-packed words can create a shortcut to mutual inspiration and understanding.

Expectations and Accountability

My daughter visited Japan a few years ago as an exchange student. Her trip was filled with fascinating experiences as she encountered Japan's fantastic culture. One of those experiences occurred on a sidewalk in Tokyo. She stopped to search for something in her tote bag, and as she rummaged through its contents, a candy wrapper fell out of the bag and landed on the ground. It was as if time stopped. Instantly, people all around her stopped to stare at the piece of litter that had fallen to the ground. My daughter knew she needed to get her trash off the ground—and fully intended to do so after she found what she was looking for in her bag.

Everyone waited.

And waited.

The tension increased with each awkward, passing second. With strangers watching her, she couldn't help but feel the immense social pressure to abandon her mission and do something that, from her point of view, was insignificant by comparison. Finally, she did just that. My daughter would never have left that trash on the ground. But her values were still prioritized differently than the sidewalk citizens who were deeply concerned about her and her litter.

Your Culture Brand will clarify expectations *and* provide the accountability to meet those expectations, and it doesn't have to be awkward. By activating the right kind of culture within our teams, that culture then promotes the right kind of accountability with metrics that everyone is aware of and understands.

Think back to that piece of litter that fell out of my daughter's bag. It may seem like an exaggerated situation, but compare it to what you might see at a typical shopping center in the United States. The expectation is that people will use the provided trash and recycle bins. But how often do you see candy wrappers, fast food wrappers, empty bottles, or other random bits of litter skittering across the sidewalks or sitting on benches right next to those receptacles? All the time! Companies hire employees whose sole job it is to pick up other people's litter. Why is that? Because while the expectation is that people will properly dispose of their trash, accountability is low.

Now, take this to the extreme. I'm sure you've seen neighborhoods where litter seems like part of the landscape. Even if a few people try to keep their yards clean, the filth that surrounds them and blows onto their property makes their efforts seem pointless. Personally, I'm thankful that no one stops to stare when someone drops a candy wrapper on the sidewalk at a shopping mall. And you probably don't want another annoying rule added to your neighborhood's homeowners' association's policy. But the fact remains that without accountability, expectations don't matter.

Organizations lose momentum when leadership allows or ignores lousy behavior. The team can regain focus if that person is removed or corrected quickly enough. If the problem behavior persists unaddressed, the team may give up on the vision altogether. In the same way, unclear expectations or a lack of accountability can make good (potentially great) team members feel defeated. If someone's efforts are continually thwarted by another employee who doesn't seem to care about the mission or the team, that person may think, *Why bother?* The impact on the organization is huge in terms of quality of work and attrition. Either the person gives up on being their best and gives in to mediocrity, or they quit and go work somewhere else where they feel like they are part of a team and their efforts matter.

A Culture Brand helps define and shape healthy cultural behavior— one that raises collective expectations, standards, and accountability, and, in turn, fosters positive momentum. It's part of that powerful wave of culture that drives the mission forward.

When accountability is missing, the tendency is to expect leaders to expend more effort holding people accountable. A healthy culture, however, creates a far more sustainable and consistent source of accountability than any micromanagement effort.

> Where in your organization might a lack of clear expectations or accountability be frustrating your team members?

Focused Vision and Clear Mission

An organization's mission, vision, and values are all supported—or under-mined—by its culture. I've noticed, for instance, that as an organization's culture improves, accountability toward achieving a shared vision is high. This happens for at least two reasons:

1. People tend to push past difficult moments or challenging situations when they have a shared vision. There's an excitement that comes when you're working toward something great with others.

2. When people share a vision, have a clear mission, *and* feel account-able to the team, organization, and their clients, they will do what-ever is within their power to support others and meet their own objectives. When there's the belief that *we're all in this together* and that every person and position matters, each person feels a sense of purpose.

Clarity is essential. Without clarity and focused effort, organizations drift off course. Think back to that illustration of the rowboat where every-one appears to be rowing in unison, but each person is rowing toward their own target—or none at all. The boat stays in motion, but requires much more effort from you, as the leader, to keep the boat aimed in the direction you want to go. Any forward movement is the average of all the targets. In this case, the average is never on target. Get clear about direction and mea-sure all efforts with that clarity.

Now, imagine that, as the leader, you weren't sure of the vision or the mission yourself. Where would your boat end up? Who knows?

That's mission drift. The contributors to the phenomenon of mission drift are a mixture of not knowing or understanding the mission and letting personalities overrule how mission gets carried out. It happens so silently that it often goes unnoticed until you end up in the metaphorical weeds along the shoreline—or completely lost. That's what happened to me.

Mission Drift

I had no idea how I'd gotten lost. As part of a family that loved nature and the great outdoors, I grew up camping and spending time in the woods. I enjoyed practicing survival skills, so when I was about nine years old, my parents gave me a compass. One day, my father and I were hiking through a small, wooded area. I had my compass with me, and I told Dad I wanted to try out my mapping skills. I assured him I knew how to read and use my trusty compass. My father knew there was a large field on the other side of the woods. We decided to split up, go in different directions, and meet on the other side. I would go straight, and he would go around. My task was to use my compass to find north and then follow the compass arrow until I came to the other side of the woods.

It seemed so simple.

I was excited for the adventure and felt grown up to be on my own. I pulled out my little compass and trudged north in my oversized boots and oversized coat. Along the way, I dodged trees, boulders, and traipsed through ravines. After I had walked for about thirty minutes, I emerged from the trees.

My father was nowhere in sight.

It took several panicky minutes for us to find one another again. Somehow, although I had found the clearing, I was nowhere near where my father expected me to meet him. I really couldn't understand it. I had done everything correctly. Or so I thought.

For years, I blamed my not-so-trusty compass for misdirecting me. When I got a little older, though, I learned how compasses work and realized my mistake. On that hike, I constantly checked to make sure the needle on my compass was pointed in the right direction. Going through a forest in a straight line, however, is impossible. That day in the woods, I went around trees and boulders and navigated ravines. In the process, I drifted. While I had consistently faced north, I sidestepped right too many times and shifted to the east without realizing it.

Later, I learned what I should have done to stay on course. Each time I pulled out my compass, I was supposed to stand still and find the correct direction. Then, I was supposed to look at the horizon and choose a landmark. This next step is the key part: Focus on moving toward the landmark before looking at the compass again. Once I reached the landmark, I could establish a new target on the horizon to move toward.

Let that sink in for a moment.

You have a goal—a vision. You set out in that direction, but distractions along the way take you off course. It happens to nine-year-old boys in the woods and corporate executives alike. The teams that I work with find themselves in the same situation. They set a clear direction and have a vision of where they're headed. They know what the mission is, but then they become so distracted by the obstacles that arise along the way that they lose sight of the target.

The solution is to take the vision and apply it to the next part of the journey. Culture Brand does that by matching individual effort to mission-driven progress.

- It helps you identify that mark on the horizon and keep it in focus.
- It is an alignment tool that provides a way to evaluate your and your team members' behavior to determine whether it is on target with the organization's core ideology (something we'll talk more about in Chapter Three).
- It is a behavior compass for those moments when someone could easily drift off course from the heart of the mission.

Some leaders default to being relational more often than making sure they are driving for results. Let's call this drifting to the right. Other leaders will be so results focused that they will miss showing care and empathy for the team. We could call this drifting to the left. If either of these is overdone, a leader could find they are way off mission. From the perspective of a team member, they feel like they are getting mixed messages about what is important. We can still over-index on one over the other, but it is now a strategic choice rather than random. We have language for the choice, and we can be prepared to compensate for meeting the mission objective.

Without this tool, it's easy to drift off course. Perhaps you've experienced something like this: You start out with a big vision and assume everyone will jump in and work together toward making it a reality. Amidst the challenge of keeping everything and everyone moving forward, chaos begins to brew. You wonder, *How did this happen? Where did we get so off course?*

Then you see it: Your vision has been reinterpreted in multiple ways. People are passionate about *their* way, *their* methods, and *their* objectives, but there is little effort to align with any sort of unified core ideology. Now, with chaos swirling all around you, getting back on course will require drastic and costly changes. It sets back your timeline considerably. Emotions run high. Some of your best people leave, and it feels like you have to start over again. That's what happens when personalities trump the priorities of the daily mission.

Managing Personalities

Teams are comprised of many different personalities—introverts and extroverts with various strengths and weaknesses. The dynamic of that variety can be beautiful and powerful. The Culture Brand framework brings people together, drawing on those strengths to work in collaboration with a unified purpose.

It's important to note that, while Culture Brand sets the expectations for behavior and creates accountability, the goal is unity, not conformity. It is, however, an excellent tool for coaching people and calling them up to the behaviors that will enable them and the people they work with to thrive.

DISC Personality Assessment

Culture Brand and personality profiles work well together. Our team at LeadersQ often uses the DISC personality assessment with new clients because it helps us understand what the person values, how they communicate, and how they are prone to react or respond to stressful situations.

D = Dominant Someone with a D personality is likely to be direct, results-oriented, strong-willed, and forceful.

I = Influence A person with a strong I personality is outgoing, optimist, enthusiastic, and full of energy. This person enjoys engaging with people.

S = Steady Someone who has a strong S personality is even-tempered, accommodating, patient, and diplomatic. This person places a high value on relationships.

C = Conscientious A person with a strong C personality is typically reserved, analytical, precise, and private.

To learn more or to take a DISC personality test, visit leadersq.com/disc-assessment-instructions

We know, for example, that someone who is a high-D according to the DISC personality assessment is direct, dominant, and decisive. They tend to be more results focused than team focused. One place this trait is likely to be apparent is when it's time to make a group decision. The fact that the person is willing to take action and to make decisions can be beneficial for the whole team—*if* they don't run over others or exclude others' voices from the decision-making process. To meet the expectations of your Culture Brand, your D-personality team member may need to find ways to increase collaboration or intentionally pause and encourage others to speak up.

Now, consider the person on the team who is a strong C personality. This person is conscientious, calculating, and highly focused on details. All of those traits can be an asset to the team—*unless* they cause the person to get stuck overanalyzing data, delay decisions, and slow the team's progress. Your C-personality team member's development plan might include involving other leaders on the team who can help them move faster on decisions.

The point isn't to *change* people's personalities but to create awareness about behaviors essential for a healthy and productive team. When you understand your team members' personalities, you can coach people to develop systems that remind them to use the essential teaming skills that don't come to them naturally. Culture Brand encourages people to grow in awareness of their bent *and* in their ability to work with and support the team, regardless of their innate personality traits. It eliminates the tendency to excuse problematic behaviors by saying, "That's just the way I am." In Part Two, we'll look at how leaders can intentionally design healthy cultures that establish a sense of purpose, community, and collaboration in cooperation with their teams so that culture drives the organization rather than those strong personalities.

A Comprehensive Tool for Your People Strategy

When someone comes into your organization, what path might they take as they move up? In many companies, the typical path to promotion is shaped by individual skill and years of experience. Each new level the person climbs up the organizational chart requires a different set of skills and demands greater responsibility.

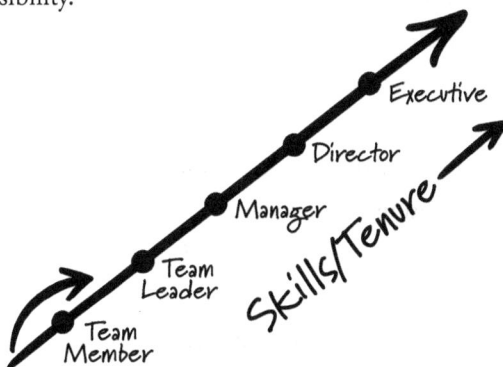

The problem with relying on these factors exclusively to determine when and to what level to promote someone takes into account only half of a team member's readiness profile. The result is that people are often promoted only to fail.

I'm sure you've experienced or know of a situation when, shortly after someone was promoted, it became obvious that it was not a good decision; they were not a good fit for the role. When this happens, it may come as a surprise that the successful team member who was given an opportunity to lead in an area of the business that they know well is now a liability to that same business area. The fact that they are a subject matter expert (SME) in that business area only makes the situation worse. If you lose that person now, the organization may lose a library of knowledge and experience. Beyond that, if you lose that person, who would be willing to take a risk of stepping into the same position?

If you've been caught in that dilemma, you may wonder what got missed along the way. Did the person change? Or did the system used to promote them fail?

In my experience, the linear approach to moving people through the organization is most often to blame. That's because growth is more like a ladder than a line.

The Ladder of Development

If we look at growth like a ladder of development, the right side represents the person's technical skills and tenure. Most businesses have metrics to inform the right side (operational skills) of the ladder. Training, tenure, production, certification, awards, and sales are easily attached to this side of talent evaluations.

The left side of the ladder represents interpersonal behaviors, including the person's emotional intelligence and cultural fit within the organization. We need a way to evaluate and develop leaders so that they can level up at each step. The challenge is that the skills on the right side of the ladder, often referred to as "hard skills," are much easier to identify, train

for, and measure. We can more easily make lists, systems, and processes for skills that are easily measured and clearly linked to operational activities. These skills can also be clarified in job descriptions and screened for in the hiring process.

The Culture Brand model adds a robust evaluation tool for the left side of the ladder of development. It establishes consistent and clear expectations and equips leaders to effectively coach team members for individual growth, promotion, and evaluation. This powerful tool also helps you to hire good-fit people because you'll know what a good cultural fit looks like. Through your screening process, you'll be able to assess if the applicant will be able to get on board with the organization's values, mission, and vision. In short, Culture Brand will help you and your team members keep the ladder balanced so they can continue to climb.

If both sides of the ladder aren't balanced, the team member is likely to fail in their new position. Most people do not exit a company, particularly those in leadership positions, because of a lack of knowledge or tenure in a business area. Most exit (or are exited) because of their behavior related to low EQ (emotional intelligence) or other behavior that is not supportive of the culture. Let me say this another way: Most people exit or are exited because of "left side of the ladder" type things. They exit or "fall off the ladder" because of left side of the ladder issues.

I was sharing this ladder example with a leadership team on the West Coast when one of the executives said, "You know, I like the ladder illustration; it helps me think about how balanced a person can move forward if they have both sides. It's like each side helps a person maintain balance."

I love that. When we're moving people in higher levels of leadership, this approach highlights the difference between navigating a tightrope and a suspension bridge. I prefer the bridge!

Culture Brand is a comprehensive tool for your people strategy, and your people strategy can then support your operational strategy by answering the following questions:

Hiring: Whom do we hire?

Onboarding: How do we describe our culture?

Developing: Where are they strong or in need of support?

Performance: What is propelling them forward, and what is getting in the way?

Correcting: Where are they struggling, and are they aware?

Disciplining: What needs immediate correction?

Rewarding: What behavior can we celebrate?

Promoting: How can we get them to the next level?

Exiting: Where have they been unwilling to grow?

Succession Planning: How do we maintain our culture through transition?

In Parts Three and Four, as we look at how to align and scale culture, we'll explore each of these pieces of your people strategy in more depth.

Culture Brand in Action: Be, Play, Win

One of our clients has identified their Culture Brand as Be, Play, Win.

Be describes **character**.

Play describes **teaming**.

Win describes **results**.

Be (Play

Win

Entry Level. At the entry-level position, the expectation of behaviors related to the Culture Brand means that they need to "Be" on time (character), they need to "Play" with a collaborative approach to their peers (teaming), and they need to strive to "Win" with excellence in their tasks (results). Notice how Be, Play, Win encompasses both the *actions* of operations and the *attitude* behind the effort.

Next Level. If a team member wants to be promoted, they have the opportunity to try some of the tasks related to the next level, but they also have the opportunity to exhibit some of the behaviors associated with that next level of responsibility. Now, rather than simply "Be" on time, they can show dependability in their personal character by having a consistently engaging attitude. They may also continue to "Play" with a collaborative approach to peers but go a step further and help support a new change in a process between teams. Inter-team communication was not expected at the base level but will be expected at the next level. If they exhibit this skill now, they are showing their readiness to move forward with more responsibility.

Roles Change. Culture Sustains.

As roles and responsibilities change as people move through the organization, your Culture Brand doesn't. The same culture transcends all positions and levels of leadership because it is founded on the values, vision, and purpose of the organization. In Part Two, we'll look at how culture can be mapped to each level or role in your organization. As we get started, we'll keep in mind that while it is okay and even necessary at times to leave behind some skills on the right side of the ladder, the behavior skills on the left are cumulative.

As a person moves up into higher skills, there is increased operational complexity and less time to maintain former operational skills. Also, in most organizations, technology changes faster at the leading edges of the organization. The leading edges are typically at the lower rungs. With promotions, there can be a distancing of skill competency. Leaders should work to understand the various skills but not seek to be proficient. It is healthy to have subject matter experts (SMEs) at each level who understand how to run a specific part of the business expertly. As leaders progress, they usually don't need to be an expert on every subject matter. They do, however, need to maintain all of their interpersonal skills, from the most basic culture behaviors to the most demanding. The values build and grow; the same behavior carries with increased responsibility and ramifications.

No matter how far you climb up the organizational chart, you never outgrow basic culture behavior. This is where a Culture Brand provides clarity for all levels of an organization. Every level is accountable to the same values behavior applied to every role and every level of responsibility.

Key Benefits of Relying on a Ladder rather than a Line

1. The ladder of development, paired with your Culture Brand, allows you to develop EveryLevel Ownership™. LeadersQ has an EveryLevel Ownership System (ELOS) for guiding the process of celebrating subject matter experts (SMEs) at every level.
2. Modeling the most basic culture behavior never loses importance.

3. Behavior can develop faster than skills. As team members' cultural behaviors improve, you can more easily spot emerging leaders.

4. Clarifying your required cultural skills opens the door for outside hiring, as these behaviors are transferable across industries and teams.

Call to Action

Draw a ladder down the middle of a piece of paper. On the right, put the heading Hard Skills, and on the left, make the heading People Skills. Take some time to list the skills, training, tenure, and other measures you use on the right side of the ladder. Then, on the left side of the ladder, make a list of requirements or responsibilities that are measured that relate to emotional intelligence and cultural expectations. This list might also include values that you expect from your team or behaviors that you do not allow in your organization.

Think about the last several people who have been exited from the organization. Circle the items on either list that contributed to them being released.

Ask yourself these questions:

1. Where is our biggest opportunity to keep people effective longer?

2. Do we have a way to develop leaders on both sides of the ladder?

3. Do we have a way to measure growth on both sides of the ladder?

Never blame the crop.

Scott stared out the passenger-side window of his father-in-law's GMC pickup, mesmerized by the rows of cotton that lined the dusty West Texas farm road, and marveled at his father-in-law's ability to plant the mile-long rows so straight each spring. Clark definitely had a gift for getting things to grow.

It was a wonder, too, that the verdant family farm seemed to stretch endlessly across the driest, flattest place on Earth. Meanwhile, back at home, his little coffee shop struggled to survive, never mind yield a profit. It seemed that every time he found great employees, they left in a matter of months. Those who didn't leave weren't great, and they were killing him with their constant drama. He had learned he couldn't count on anyone to show up on time to open or stay until closing, which meant he was working long days—and still not getting everything done.

He'd left a perfectly comfortable corporate job to pursue his dream of owning his own business. The service industry, specifically something that allowed him to interact with people, seemed like a good fit for his personality. He had this dream of getting to know his regulars and building a place that felt like an extension of home.

Culture Brand

Over the years, his coffee habit had turned into a hobby, and he discovered he had a knack for roasting coffee and creating interesting blends. Combining his passion for people, his love for coffee, and his expertise in operations made the decision to open The Coffee Nook simple. Within no time, he found a good location in an older (almost historical) home near downtown of his metro-area bedroom community. And when he opened the doors, his coffee got great reviews. Unfortunately, his passion for serving the best coffee in town wasn't translating into profits, and he was beginning to understand why.

Everything about setting up a business had been so solvable. Everything except in the area of talent. He liked to think the best of people and wanted to give anyone willing to work hard a chance to be part of his team. But he didn't see how he could call it a team. *He* was the team. Everyone who worked for him seemed to be either underperforming operationally or overperforming and running off other team members. He had tried to pick up the slack, but it just wasn't working.

For the past few months, sales had gone down month over month. If that trend continued... well, he didn't want to think about that.

Instead, he told himself that business had just slowed down for the summer. People were traveling. They'd be back.

He hoped.

Summer didn't seem to be an issue on Clark's farm. The cotton plants were thriving despite the brutal heat or the fact that not a single tree broke the horizon to offer shade from the sun or shelter from the sweeping winds.

It was his wife, Emma, who suggested, or rather insisted, that he close the shop for a couple of weeks so they could get away and spend time with her family. She had grown up out here and hoped Scott could find a way to lose some stress in the fields.

Inspecting the crops was one of Clark's weekly habits. He'd invited Scott to "help," which basically meant keeping the older man company while he drove the dusty roads through the fields. Truthfully, the quiet routines of the farm had been rejuvenating. Clark had plenty of stories to share, but the man was also happy to let silence fall between them as they enjoyed the scenery. If Emma had told her dad that there was any trouble with Scott's business, then he hadn't let on. Which was fine with Scott. He was sure that if he could just get away, recover from the stress of dealing with all the frustrations of work, he'd be ready to jump back into the craziness when he returned.

The truck rolled to a stop. Clark gazed out over the rows for a few seconds before getting out.

Scott watched as Clark started up one of the rows. Curious, he climbed out of the truck and followed his father-in-law a few yards into the field of knee-high cotton. There, Clark pulled out a pocket-knife and knelt on the dry, sandy dirt. Scott bent, hands on his knees, and observed as Clark used the knife to cut a pod off the plant and then slice open the cotton boll, the early forming fruit of the plant.

The plants themselves were green and leafy, but even Scott could tell a difference between these immature bolls and those they had seen elsewhere on the farm. "What's wrong with these plants?" he asked.

Straightening up, he shielded his eyes with his hand and scanned the surrounding fields. "It looks like the problem covers several acres."

Clark snapped his knife closed and pushed himself up. "My daddy used to say, 'Never blame the crop for a poor harvest.'"

Rather than respond, Scott just nodded. He had no idea what that meant but opted to keep his mouth shut rather than prove himself a certified city boy. He wasn't blaming the plants. He just wanted to understand what had happened here when the rest of the crop looked so good.

Clark pulled a bandana from his back pocket, removed his hat long enough to mop the sweat from his face, then tucked the dampened cloth away. "This here's a low spot. It tends to hold water when it rains. Shortly after I planted this spring, we had quite a bit of rain, and a small lake formed here." He swept his arm from one side of the field to the other, gesturing to the affected area.

Scott followed Clark when he turned and ambled back to the truck. "We need the water, obviously," his father-in-law continued. "But too much water makes the soil soggy. It stunts young cotton plants."

"So what do you do about it?" Scott wondered aloud. He knew that every acre counted when it came time to harvest. Surely Clark wouldn't just write off the whole field as a loss.

When they'd reached the truck, Clark paused and surveyed the field once more. "Great crops come from great soil. The best way to care for the crop is to care for the soil, so that's what we're gonna do. I took some soil samples last week and talked with the local ag extension office. They had some suggestions about how to get these plants growing like they should."

"That sounds like a lot of extra work."

Clark chuckled and shook his head as he walked around to his side of the cab. "Some, for sure. But the way I see it, it's better to put in a little extra work than to lose the whole field. Especially if we can get the field to produce like it should."

They climbed back into the dusty pickup and continued their rounds. As the rows of cotton flashed by, Clark's comments replayed in Scott's mind: "Great crops come from great soil. The best way to care for the crop is to care for the soil."

I'm not thriving. I'm barely surviving.

Never blame the crop. Care for the soil so the crop can thrive.

Whether Clark meant to or not, he had given Scott something to think about.

If I want the business to grow, I've got to create the right environment.

Never blame the crop.

Scott had lost himself in the story and the memories of how far his business had come in the three years since that visit to Clark's farm. He paused and looked around the conference room. The modern space in the downtown Houston skyscraper was far removed from his cozy coffee shop—and farther still from those cotton fields.

His story had resonated with Kate that day in the coffee shop, and he could tell that a few people sitting at the table got it. Others, however, made him wonder what he was doing there and if his experience could make a difference here. A few appeared confused or skeptical. One stared at him, arms crossed, with an expression that bordered on hostile.

That look told him it was time to wrap things up. "My business wasn't thriving because my team wasn't thriving. And it wasn't until that afternoon with my father-in-law that I realized it wasn't their fault that we were struggling," Scott said. "As the leader, it is my job to create the right environment for growth."

"Thank you, Scott." Kate met him at the front of the conference room. "I appreciate you coming here to share your experience."

Scott nodded and sat in one of the leather chairs that surrounded the massive table.

Kate addressed her team of executive leaders. "I wanted you to hear Scott's story because I think we need to ask ourselves some of the same questions he asked. Questions like, What environment am I asking my team to work in? Is this a place that encourages people to thrive?

"Our team has already worked hard to establish our core ideology. We've outlined our purpose, values, mission, and vision. For some reason, however, we are still not moving forward together. It occurred to me after Scott told me about the changes he'd made to his business that we have a disconnect between our ideology and our efforts—and that gap is negatively impacting our people and our outcomes. We need to think like a team and work together."

Again, Scott noticed a few people nodding. A couple seemed preoccupied with their phones.

Hostile-guy let out a huff of irritation and suddenly had the attention of everyone in the room. "That was a fun farm story. Thanks, Scott." The man's tone belied disdain rather than gratitude. "Kate, I get that you're drowning and you think that this culture stuff is a way to right your sinking ship, but don't you think we've had way too many team-building exercises this year already?"

Wow, Scott thought. *Hostile's the word, all right.* Even as an out-sider, he could tell that *team* was not in this guy's vocabulary.

All eyes shifted to Kate.

"Actually, I don't know if 'team-building exercises' are exactly what we need, Ryan. But I do think to right our ship, it's going to take all of us working together," Kate replied.

Ryan shook his head as he looked at his watch. "What I know is that I have work to do if I'm going to hit my targets."

Kate opted to ignore his comment and turned her focus to the VPs, who seemed a little more engaged. "What Scott has done to build his team's culture could give us some insights into how we can get everyone moving together to accomplish our mission." Kate offered a weary smile and checked her watch. "I truly believe we have a bright future, but we must find a way to create a win-ning culture. It is our job to tend the soil, so to speak, if we want a rich harvest.

"Right now, though, I think it's time for a break. Let's take fif-teen minutes. When we come back, Scott, I'd love for you to share a little more."

The group dispersed to refuel on coffee and catch up on emails. Kate let out a small sigh and sat in the chair beside him. Scott heard her say under her breath, "I hope this works."

Never blame the crop.

"I'm going to step out for a minute too," Scott said. Truthfully, he wanted to bolt. Instead, he left the room, walking as calmly as he could. But his mind raced with doubts. *That did* not *go well.* It was obvious Kate's leaders were struggling to connect with his story. *How does anything I have to offer relate to what they are doing here? What am I doing here?*

He found a quiet space and sent a text to his wife.

Scott:

> I'm not sure this was a good idea.

Emma:

> What's wrong?

> I don't belong here. I'm the owner of a tiny coffee shop with some crazy farm stories! I don't think I connected with them.

> Remember, Kate asked you to tell your story. She didn't ask you to transform her team.

> You're right. I'm just not much of a public speaker.

> Not yet. But you are a good storyteller. Just tell your story. Remember, you're a guest at a farm that is not your own. Kate is responsible for the results.

> Thank you! I'm gonna take a walk and refocus. You're amazing!

Emma's encouragement sparked a memory that Scott needed right now—an embarrassing moment on the farm when he made a huge mess of things by losing his focus. Clark got him through it and taught him a valuable lesson. It was a story Kate's team needed to hear.

CHAPTER 2
Led by Design—or Default

Culture is action, not words.

—Jason Fried

Culture happens, either by design or by default. Left to chance, culture will always drift toward chaos—into toxicity at worst and dysfunction at best. Un-led cultures follow the path of least resistance. They are governed by the strongest personalities and personal preferences rather than priorities. Even well-designed culture can become fractured and divided without consistent leadership, particularly when personalities override priorities. In either case, the result is chaos. Team members are left to decide on their own who or what is right when they hear conflicting messages about what is important.

In contrast, when you *design* your Culture Brand with intention and purpose based on your core ideology, you build a system for ownership and success at every level of the organization. Part of designing a Culture Brand is identifying behaviors that align with and support the organization's mission, vision, and values. Like a "law," these behaviors supersede personal behavior biases. They also ensure that your team members know how to climb the ladder of development.

So who is responsible for these laws?

You are.

Leadership is about creating order from chaos, and one of the key responsibilities of a leader is to establish a growth environment where people thrive as productive members of a team. The reality is that's a big job. Being in leadership is challenging—more challenging than emerging or even more experienced leaders who are taking new roles might expect. It's harder still without a culture design in place. Before we focus on what it looks like for your culture to be led by design, let's look at what happens when it isn't.

A State of Chaos

Your team members represent a variety of motivations, and sometimes, people simply don't want to follow. As we saw in the previous chapter, when culture isn't directed, personalities and personal preferences tend to drive behavior. Add to that the fact that each person has their own perspective about their contribution to the organization's goals, and it's no wonder that people end up rowing in different directions.

Sometimes, however, it's success that takes the team off course. Success is a good thing, but keeping up with growth often requires adding team members, which can lead to misalignment. Here's how: Small teams and founding teams typically know the cultural norms because, written or unwritten, they helped create them. As a team grows, the assumption can be that the new hires will automatically understand those cultural norms; after all, these norms are implicit. They are "just the way we do things." Working under this assumption means that fissures often go unnoticed until the gap in alignment is glaringly wide. The original mission, along with the good intentions of that implicit, unwritten culture that was formed by the initial team, gets lost as new personalities come on board. Segmented cultures form to create an *us*-versus-*them* environment that divides the organization. Fissures become fault lines that incite fear in the best of leaders.

When founders and CEOs notice a gap that formed quietly has become a chasm, their next move is crucial—and it's often the wrong one. The tendency is to react to the deep divisions and crumbling loyalty by frantically jumping deep into the business on a culture rescue mission using the tools and strategies that worked when the company was significantly smaller. This frantic and fear-driven approach is stressful for everyone and often adds more chaos than order to the team.

Here's what that looks like:

1. Getting shoulder to shoulder in the work to rescue morale
2. Focusing on 1:1 meetings with leaders at all levels to engage everyone personally
3. Listening to needs or concerns and looking for quick wins and ways to solve problems quickly
4. Creating forums for listening sessions to lead the charge for rebuilding buy-in

None of these actions is *bad*; in fact, some or all of them may be necessary. But the founder methods that worked well in the early days with a smaller, close-knit team will have a different impact now. A leader who jumps in like this often creates more confusion, undermines established leaders, and subverts standard operations and procedures. Founders and C-suite executives who overreact with their original culture-building methods risk alienating their most faithful leaders as they seek to get new leaders on board. The business's complexity at this mature stage calls for a different approach to culture transformation, one that creates clarity and equips all levels of leadership with a unified cultural message. From there, the leadership *team* is empowered to guide the organization into alignment.

Be a Chief Culture Officer

The highest executive positions of an organization are often called the C-suite. At this level, the C, which stands for *chief* in CEO, CSO, CMO, CPO, CFO, etc., implies that the person holding the title is the top leader of that business segment.

My challenge to the chief executive officers (CEOs) I coach is to think of themselves primarily as chief culture officers. Reframing a role that traditionally overemphasizes execution and result-focused leadership is a mindset shift with a profound impact. As chief culture officers, leaders aim higher than just execution. By focusing on organizational culture, they make the success target the nexus of results, relationships, and personal character. A chief culture officer leads with all three essential elements of Culture Brand in mind: results, teaming, and character.

With the mindset of a chief culture officer and the comprehensive nature of Culture Brand, you pave the way for healthy growth—for your team, for your leaders, and for the organization.

Designing a Winning Culture

I have been consulting with leaders since 2012, helping them and their teams unravel bad behavior and build healthy cultures so they can win together. I have seen teams in many different conditions, from thriving to barely surviving.

What I have noticed is that the toxic behavior of unhealthy teams almost always skews one of two ways. Either the focus leans heavily toward results with a win-at-all-costs mentality, or the push to maintain peace and protect relationships is so strong that no one is willing to rock the boat with any sort of conflict.

Mark Miller, the former vice president of high-performance leadership at Chick-fil-A, famously asked, "Which is the most important word in the phrase: results and relationships?" The answer is *and*. These two competing drivers, results *and* relationships, are both essential. Businesses need to deliver results to survive. At the same time, teams are made of people, and people thrive on relationships. For results-focused leaders, however, investing in the relational aspects of teams feels weak or oversensitive and emotional. But if teams focus exclusively on results, the wins become hollow victories, and employee engagement diminishes. Leaders and teams that put too much emphasis on relationships are no better off. When teams avoid conflict to the point that they neglect or impede essential execution, they don't get results. These teams eventually fail or get outpaced by competition. Either scenario is full of the conflict they've worked so hard to avoid.

High-performance teams deliver both solid results and strong relationships. If you've ever been part of a high-performance team, you know that creating the kind of atmosphere that fosters a high-performance team culture requires intentionality. Culture happens by default, but a winning culture only happens by design.

Moving Toward Health

Unhealthy teams are costly. They slow performance and accelerate turnover. Unfortunately, the most toxic players on the team are often the last to exit the organization. The best are some of the first to leave.

> Culture happens by default, but a winning culture only happens by design.

Early on in my consulting, I devoted a lot of time and energy to identifying and addressing toxic behaviors. It felt more like surgery than growth. With every new client company, I followed a similar plan of attack:

1. Listen in and observe team problems.
2. Help teams diagnose the significant dysfunctions.
3. Work to help them reconcile deep conflicts.
4. Identify a strategy or action plan forward.
5. Work through fixing dysfunctional habits.

We had many successes and breakthroughs, but the approach was more about effectively managing the symptoms than solving the root causes. Honestly, the burden of trying to *fix* unhealthy teams felt heavy. These struggling organizations needed help, and I wondered if there was a better way to move forward with results *and* win at teaming.

Shifting the focus away from treating the symptoms of team dysfunction and instead prioritizing creating and nurturing healthy teams proved to be the answer. Rather than putting so much energy into diagnosing and addressing toxic behavior, we developed strategies to build the kind of culture we wanted. We picked targets to move toward rather than looking back at what we didn't want. With Culture Brand, I am advocating that teams can overcome most dysfunction by moving toward healthy culture.

Although diagnostic and surgical work are no longer my starting point, they are still necessary. It's essential to get brutally honest in our reflections. When things aren't working, two fundamental questions have to be answered:

- What is wrong here?
- What is keeping us from winning together?

If the answers point to specific people, we can coach them to grow in EQ or help them unlearn some negative habits related to team dynamics. Not everyone will be willing to change within the timeline required, but sometimes they will. And when that happens, it's a win for everyone.

Understanding EQ

Emotional Quotient (EQ) is understanding yourself and others. Honestly, it takes a lifetime to do either. We develop EQ over time, through self-reflection and observing how we interact with our environment. Questions like those below are a good place to start:

- How do I respond to stress?
- What happens when I'm in a crowd of people?
- What methods do I use to make decisions?
- What are some of my social fears?

The EQ insights gained through this kind of reflection help us understand the predictable aspects of our personality. Applying those same kinds of questions to the people around us can help us understand predictable patterns in their behavior.

Emotional Intelligence takes both self and others into account and uses that information to interact more successfully in life and with others.

A Rally Point

In the days before cell phones, whenever our family went to an amusement park, we established a rally point and check-in time before going in separate directions. No matter where we went in the park, we would gather at a specific time to make sure everyone was doing well—safe, hydrated, and wearing plenty of sunscreen.

Cultures need rally points, too, and your Culture Brand is the rally point that everyone can move toward. Defining the boundaries of and goals for behavior makes it easier for team members to represent or participate in the defined culture. Calling the team to live up to the culture's values and holding everyone accountable to those values keeps the organization working in alignment.

Will You Join Me on This Journey?

As you move through this book, we'll get specific on how you can make your culture tangible and accessible to everyone: clearly defined, measurable, and winnable. Your Culture Brand will transform how everyone talks about being part of your team. It will instill confidence in their personal ownership and leadership. You'll watch your team members come together to reach goals that seemed impossible and grow closer as a community as they work to accomplish a shared mission.

It is going to require the best of you to *design* your desired culture, *align* your team around that vision, and then *scale* your culture to the entire organization. When doubts as to whether it's worth it or whether it's working creep in, pause and say to yourself, "I am responsible for my team culture. I am a culture leader."

It's worth it.

Culture matters.

Culture gets results.

Winning culture happens by design.

Get to Higher Ground

*"A leader in quicksand is not thinking about culture.
They need to get to the high ground."*
—Mark Miller

I count Mark Miller as a friend and mentor. Each time I've had the privilege of being in the same room with him, I've left refreshed and inspired by his leadership. Mark is the author of eleven leadership books, and one of his most recent, *Culture Rules*, came out just before he retired from a long career at Chick-fil-A as vice president of high-performance leadership. In *Culture Rules*, Mark identifies three steps to helping grow a culture.

1. Eliminate toxins.
2. Choose to double down on a strength.
3. Add new capabilities.

It's excellent advice, and it is exactly what *Culture Brand* can help you accomplish. As you clarify the behaviors you want and *don't* want to see in your organization, you identify the toxic behavior to eliminate as well as the strengths that you want to double down on. And finally, it reveals the gaps where you need new capabilities.

As Mark describes the move toward leaders' responsibility for culture transformation, he says, "A leader in quicksand is not thinking about culture. They need to get to the high ground."

With Culture Brand, you can establish and define the high ground. And my hope is that you'll grab hold and use this powerful tool to pull yourself out of the quicksand. I want you to be able to say, "We are winning at culture, and our culture is helping us win."

Call to Action

The next chapter focuses on your core ideology, your purpose, values, mission, and vision. Before you dive in, take a few minutes to gather any of those statements that you have already created for your organization.

Review your existing messaging. Ask yourself these questions:

1. Is our message clear?

2. Is our message compelling?

3. What top three team behaviors keep us from accomplishing our core ideology?

What markers could help us get on track and stay on target?

Like every smart business owner, Scott had created a business plan before opening his shop. But after securing a business loan and opening the coffee shop, that document and all his big plans were quickly buried under the daily work of putting out fires. It was Clark and the unexpected, MBA-worthy insights he gained on the family farm that pushed **him** to remember why he was in business and what he really wanted to accomplish.

Out at the farm three years earlier, Clark's solution for Scott's doldrums was to put him to work, driving a tractor—something Scott had never done before. His lack of experience didn't deter Clark from tasking him with plowing one of the forty-acre fields.

"We'll be fighting sand today," Clark said. "This dry, sandy soil is exactly what cotton thrives in. The problem is, when we get a bit of rain, the sand turns into a thin layer of mud and then crusts up in a hard shell when the sun comes out. When the wind blows in, it kicks up grains of sand that blast the cotton, slicing right through the stalks."

Clark walked Scott to the back of the tractor and rested his hand on the strut of the plow. Twelve giant blades were attached to the back of the tractor. "This is how we fight the sand. These blades dig into the soil and break up the crust. But you've gotta be careful as you drive. If you don't keep your rows straight, you'll cut right through the plants." The older man chuckled and moved toward the tractor's cab. "That'd defeat the whole purpose."

Clark's instructions were clear and simple: "Keep one hand on the steering wheel and the other hand near these two levers," he said, pointing to the throttle and, next to it, the lever that controlled the plow depth. Scott wished Clark had given him a bit more instruction before turning him loose on the fields, but that wasn't how Clark operated. He was more of a learn-as-you-go type of teacher. Before he left, Clark said, "It's relaxing work. Gives a person time to think." With that, he shut the cab door and sent Scott on his way.

So there he was, driving a tractor for the first time in his life. As the giant machine bumped along the sandy earth, Scott had to admit that he could see how plowing fields might be relaxing—if you had years of experience. Instead, the task of keeping the blades positioned between the long rows seemed daunting. It was necessary work, though, and he didn't want to let Clark down.

Scott focused on a dent in the front left corner of the tractor. "Find a spot on the tractor and match it to a straight row. As long as you maintain that, you'll drive straight as an arrow," Clark had told him. It really felt a lot easier said than done. He felt like he was going straight, but was he?

Scott turned his head to look at the plow behind him. It seemed to be pretty good for a city boy. The blades were missing the cotton entirely. Scott allowed himself a small smile—until he noticed the harrow was drifting to the right. Scott watched five feet of cotton rows get mown down before he whipped his head forward and jerked the tractor wheel over to the left to get back on course. He looked back again and saw that the blades were off to his left now.

What markers could help us get on track and stay on target?

The immaculately straight rows of cotton looked as if a toddler had visited a Zen garden.

Panicking, Scott grabbed the lever to slow down, hoping to stop the destruction. He sighed with relief as the tractor slowed, then gasped at the grinding sound coming from behind him. In his haste to slow the tractor, he accidentally grabbed the lever that lowered the blades. The knives dropped deep into the soil, causing the tractor to lurch as it fought against the earth. He quickly found the throttle and pulled the tractor to a stop. He tried using the lever to lift the blades, but they refused to budge.

Scott opened the door and hopped out to survey the damage. Countless young cotton plants lay dead behind him. The rows that had been immaculately straight were bent into a terrible zigzag shape. And the tractor was stuck in the middle of the field with its huge blades buried in the deep sand.

How had this happened? Scott mentally kicked himself as Clark's advice came to mind. "Find a mark on the tractor and match it to a straight row. Stay on that line." Scott knew exactly how it had happened: he'd gotten distracted and taken his eye off the mark.

He had to get the knives unstuck. But how? Noticing a small shovel strapped to the toolbox, he grabbed it and started digging out the first blade. It was deep. He was going to have to call Clark.

Clark arrived about thirty minutes later on his own tractor and assessed the situation. He was surprisingly calm. Not a smile and not a frown. He stepped down from his tractor and grabbed two larger shovels that he had evidently picked up from the barn on the way to Scott's rescue.

"Son, that looks pretty stuck. It'll take some time to dig it out before the lift can pull free without breaking the blades," he said.

Then, without further comment, Clark handed Scott one of the shovels. The two worked side by side in silence until they'd freed the blades.

When they'd finished, Scott thanked Clark. The man simply nodded as he climbed into his tractor and said, "You're all set. I'll see you back at the barn when you're done."

No rebuke. No correction. Just an opportunity to be trusted again and finish the field.

Back in his tractor, Scott kept his pace steady—and a little slower. He lined up the nose of the tractor with a specific row and kept the blades precisely in the right spot between the evenly spaced cotton plants. Whenever he needed to look over his shoulder to the field behind him, or even just to check the blades on either side, he throttled down first. Eventually, he felt comfortable increasing his speed and was able to finish the field.

A few hours later, the men quietly ate a late lunch together near the well house back at the barn. Scott admired Clark's steady, calm demeanor. He had destroyed months of work with his costly mistake, but Clark never showed any concern. Instead, his father-in-law just showed up to help get him out of a jam.

That's when Scott realized two things. The first was how incredibly easy it was to get off track. The mess he had created in the field mirrored what he saw every day in the coffee shop. He had all the right elements in place—he knew where the business was going and why it existed—but just like in the field, mistakes happened quickly when he took his eyes off the guiding markers. The other, more significant thing he learned was that with a simple set of guidelines, he could recover and get back on track.

He needed something similar for his team: a simple way for them to know, moment by moment, whether they were on mission and moving in the right direction. He didn't know it yet, but he was only days away from a discovery that would change everything. Clark's advice echoed in his mind. If a tractor needed clear lines to stay on course, then his team needed clear markers, too. He already knew the *why* and the *what* of his business; now, he needed a way to articulate the *how*—how to stay on mission minute by minute. *What markers could help us get on track and stay on target?* If he could get everyone moving in the right direction, they'd have a much better chance not only of keeping the doors open but of building the kind of business he had always envisioned.

Scott's second realization was that he had work to do with his team, not just in terms of training but also in building trust. He thought about the costly mistakes that kept piling up—wasted product, customers frustrated by slow service or wrong orders, negative reviews, and good employees growing disenchanted by coworkers' drama or incompetence. In addition to finding a way to help his team focus on the right actions, Scott knew he had to learn how to redirect them intentionally without alienating them with his own disappointment. Clark's encouragement and display of trust after Scott had created such a mess had allowed him to try again and finish the job successfully. Trust was a gift. And it had to be nurtured. Blame, not trust, had become something of a habit around The Coffee Nook. If he weren't careful, Scott knew blame would destroy the trust his team had in him and in one another.

A few weeks after Scott's visit to the office, Kate gathered her executive team for a two-day, off-site meeting. As she prepped for the retreat, she recalled his story about getting stuck in the cotton field—and how Clark had handled it. The problems she faced with her team weren't all that different than those Scott dealt with at his coffee shop—although the financial stakes and lives that would be affected if the company didn't get on track soon were significantly higher.

It had taken some convincing to get her leaders to take the time away from the office. Several complained that they had a retreat only two months earlier. Like this one, that retreat had been important. She'd had a consultant come in and coach the leadership through the process of clarifying the company's mission, vision, and values. The process had been valuable. It had also been somewhat arduous, so her leaders' reluctance didn't surprise her.

Since then, however, it had become obvious that although the company's mission and vision were clear, her leaders seemed either ill-equipped or unwilling to enforce the daily changes that would be necessary to stay on course. And it was clear that, although they had identified specific values by which to operate, at least a few of her leaders (and by default, their teams) thought it was okay to ignore them for the sake of their own success.

The frustrating part in all of this was that she knew her leadership team had the necessary talent and technical expertise to help the company hit its income and reach its objectives. Ability wasn't the issue.

In the past few weeks, she had identified a few problems that she hoped the culture transformation would resolve.

First, although everyone seemed to be working to achieve the mission, each department was siloed. The lack of open communication inhibited cohesive effort. The effect was that the systems were clunky. Everything took longer than it should because, invariably, one department or another didn't have the resources or information necessary to take the next steps. This led to a second problem: back-channels and workarounds.

Some of her leaders and their teams habitually circumvented proper channels of communication and ignored standard operating procedures. When she addressed the issue, those leaders told her it was the only way to hit their targets. (Ryan, who headed production, was one of the worst offenders when it came to SOPs. But he certainly wasn't alone.) The trouble was that the workarounds too often sabotaged other teams.

What markers could help us get on track and stay on target?

To hit their quarterly targets, the sales team would make promises that production couldn't keep. Marketing launched initiatives without the input of the sales and customer service teams, which often led to complaints from clients and confusion on the sales team. In an effort to placate angry clients, customer service drained any profit by issuing returns and blindly accepting cancellations rather than offering solutions that would satisfy and maintain the customer.

Every leader seemed to be more focused on their team's success than on the success of the organization as a whole. The result was constant conflict between department leaders. Every day, she had at least one new fire to put out. With all the chaos, she found it impossible to get her own work done at the office, which was why she often worked late into the evening after she'd put her children to bed.

She needed her leaders to understand—and be able to communicate to their teams—that each department played a critical role in the company's success. To achieve Intelex's mission and vision, everyone would have to work together. This habit of working against one another, whether it was deliberate or by default, would have to stop.

The reality of knowing that the company could fail if things didn't change weighed heavily on Kate. She, along with potentially hundreds of her employees, would be out of a job. Kate knew she couldn't let that happen. She felt an obligation to the board, her leaders, their teams—and herself.

Just like every other leader on her executive team, Kate wanted to win. Something Scott had said that day in the coffee shop had made her acutely aware of her drive for results. Bill had pointed out that quality about her as well. Great results were what winning meant to her. That was her motivation—and everyone knew it. But she also valued integrity. So as much as she wanted to win, she wanted to do it in the right way—a way that honored the people on her team, the shareholders, and the clients.

Culture Brand

In her preparation for the off-site, she had taken time to evaluate each of her leaders. As she did, she realized that each one of them had unique motivations and values. And not all of them were in alignment with the company's mission and values statements that were painted on the lobby walls in their building.

Revisiting those values and goals was the first order of business for the off-site. It was one thing to claim integrity as a value. But she had learned in recent months that not everyone understood what it meant to live out that value in their daily operations—especially when people felt pressured to succeed. That's where Scott's idea of *designing* culture came in. If they were going to win as a team, they needed a way to make their values actionable and measurable.

She needed everyone to be on board if this culture transformation was going to work. She just hoped they would be receptive to this simple concept that would make their core ideology tangible and measurable—and could keep the team aligned moment by moment.

CHAPTER 3

PV²M + Culture Brand

Culture is influenced significantly by the values of the organization's leadership. These are not the written values, but the "lived" values.

—David McNally

In their book *Built to Last,* Jim Collins and Jerry I. Porras popularized the term *core ideology*. It's a term that comprises the driving force behind a winning organization: core values, a core purpose, and a Big Hairy Audacious Goal (BHAG). A company's core ideology defines an organization and points it in a strategic and inspiring direction.

I consider developing your core ideology pre-work to designing your Culture Brand because it provides the foundation from which you can ask and answer the questions necessary to create unity, identity, and success. When my clients and I do this work together, we start by exploring purpose, values, vision, and mission before we look at where Culture Brand fits in. Chances are good that your organization has already identified at least some of the elements of your culture ideology, but in the interest of creating a common language, let's take a quick look at each one.

Purpose, Values, Vision, and Mission

Imagine driving down an old country road that has a ditch running along each side. You must stay on the road as you wind through the hay fields and pastures. You know you would get stuck in the ditch if you veered off the road to the left or the right.

These ditches are clear boundaries that keep you focused on staying on the road and traveling safely toward your destination.

These boundaries in our core ideology are **purpose** and **values**. They are the guideposts that keep us on the right path. No matter where the road takes us, purpose and values keep us aligned.

Way up ahead on the horizon of this country road is your **vision**. Vision is a picture of the future. It is where you are going.

The road itself represents your **mission**. Your mission defines the regular and consistent action necessary to keep you moving forward. If you stay on mission, aligned with your values and purpose, you'll continue that forward progress.

So what does clarifying your core ideology have to do with culture? Everything! The culture you are building needs a clear core ideology or organizational roadmap so people can follow as they travel with you. Before you get in the car, you need to identify why you're embarking on the journey in the first place, how you will navigate the road ahead, where you want to go, and what you'll do when you arrive.

Get as clear as possible on what composes your core ideology, then determine which aspects are nonnegotiable. A lot can happen on a long journey, but if you can answer why, how, where, and what, you can jump in the vehicle and know that you are well-prepared for the journey ahead.

Purpose

Remember, your purpose is one of those boundaries. When your purpose is clear, it guides you to stay on mission.

So how do you decide what your purpose is? One way to find your purpose is to answer the question, *why?* As in, *Why do I exist?* or *Why does this business exist?*

Asking *why* will help you discover or clarify your purpose. It's a powerful question you must answer.

Note: This is a question you, as the leader, must ask yourself, but if you are doing this exercise with a leader on your team, make sure your motives are clearly stated. Asking why of those below you on the organizational chart can come across as judgmental: "Why would you do that?"

Five Whys

One technique developed by Taiichi Ohno, the father of the Toyota Production System, to get past the surface whys and find the real answer—and also referenced in Eric Ries's 2011 *Lean Startup*—is the "Five Whys." After warning my client that we're going to dig deep (and possibly get annoying) by repeatedly asking *why*, a coaching conversation focused on purpose might sound something like this:

Me: Why do you have this accounting business? (Why #1)

Client: To serve our customers.

Me: Why do you want to serve customers? (Why #2)

Client: Because we enjoy serving people.

Me: Why do you enjoy serving people, and why accounting specifically? (Why #3)

Client: Well, we see people who are struggling with their taxes and accounting. We know they need our help, and we have this expertise.

Me:	OK, why do you want to help people who are struggling with their finances? (Why #4)
Client:	Because they feel alone and are never really sure whether their finances are correct or if they have to worry about losing money or getting audited.
Me:	Why do you want to serve people who worry that their finances might be incorrect or in trouble? (Why #5)
Client:	We don't want our clients to feel alone. We want them to be confident in their financial decisions.
Me:	Bingo! That's what we are looking for. That's purpose.

They had done it. This team found their real *why*. They wanted their clients to be confident in their financial decisions. Having this deeper version of their purpose helps inform their values and define their mission. Once they have determined their purpose, values, and mission, they can look into the future and imagine a great vision. The core ideology arrow is complete.

When you ask *why* this many times, you'll discover that your purpose runs much deeper than money or even providing a valuable service. My clients often get emotional and very present with that final *why* as they reflect on the needs of the people they serve. This technique helps them focus and zero in on their *real* purpose. With this deeper insight, the daily activities of the mission tend to feel more meaningful and less mundane.

If you are a leader, you need to know not only the organization's purpose but also *your* why—the purpose you serve with your life and within the organization. Your personal *why* must somehow align with the purpose of the organization you are serving. If your *why* isn't in strong alignment with the company's purpose, you'll find it difficult to move the business forward. The same is true for your values.

Purpose is bigger than any mission. It should hardly change in your lifetime, and it can span over many different types of missions that you may be actively pursuing. Mission changes based upon the situation or application of the purpose; for example, what if you know your purpose is to relieve suffering on the earth? That purpose does not have a metric attached to it, nor does it have a specific methodology, but it can guide any number of missions. You might feed the homeless while working with an urban nonprofit. Down the road, perhaps you earn a medical degree and travel to rural areas where healthcare options are scarce. Later, you may take a leadership position with a global organization serving orphans. Your mission would have changed with each career transition, but your purpose remained constant.

Purpose is your reason for existing. Ask *why*.

- Why does your business exist?

- Why does your work matter?

- Why do your clients need you?

- What is *your* personal purpose?

Values

Purpose runs along one side of the metaphorical road of your organization's mission. Values serve as the boundary on the other side of that road. Our values guide us. That's true for individuals and for organizations. It's also true regardless of whether our values are good or not-so-good. And just as organizations and individuals need to know their purpose, they need to clearly define their desired values.

Most of the time, when it's time to talk about values, the go-to practice is to pull out a list of *value* words and choose a few appealing words. But there is more to defining the values that we want to drive our organizations and lives; this takes more than selecting nice or popular words from someone else's list.

When working with organizations, I find it helps to identify values in (at least) three different categories:

1. Permission-to-Play Values
2. Distinguishing Values
3. Deeply Held Values

Permission-to-play values are those characteristics *every* business should strive to exhibit; for example, integrity and trust. One would hope that all businesses operate with integrity. In other words, these are not unique values. We should be able to find these values in every business. Most communities and client bases expect these and do not treat them as special or surprising. These are traits that should be essential to any business in the way they interact with customers, deal with employee disputes, or handle finances.

Since permission-to-play values should be everywhere, we typically discourage companies from choosing from this category for their cultural ideology. If you still want to use a word like *integrity* as a value in your business, however, it will be important for you and your employees to understand exactly how this value applies to the work you do. You will need to elevate and interpret the definition and application of that word. If you are a home builder, for example, one way you might define integrity is with the commitment to building homes that stand strong for one hundred years or homes that are built with the highest standards inside and out.

Distinguishing values are those that apply specifically to your industry, your country, your local community, or a subculture created by your customers. Distinguishing values push your organization to stand out among competitors. These are what some might call "extra mile" values. They are values that still make business sense but go beyond normal effort within similar organizations.

As I'm writing, Southwest Airlines is undergoing an operational overhaul, but their current values statement includes the discipline values: Be safe, Be focused, and Be reliable. These are distinguishing values in the airline industry and make sense for successful business operations. Some of their other values, like "Act like an owner" and "Kick tail," may belong in the next category.

Deeply held values are unique to and so ingrained into your organization's makeup that your customers, vendors, and employees can't help but notice them. These values make your business stand out in your community or industry.

Many times, deeply held values are traits that have been present from the very early days of a company's existence. This category of values may appear counterintuitive to the industry. Such is the case with Panda Express. When Andrew Cherng and his father, Master Chef Ming Tsai Cherng, opened their first restaurant in 1972, business was slow. To Andrew, the slow growth meant each new guest was something to be grateful for. Andrew expressed his gratitude with generosity.

"We didn't have many guests; we were not making much money, but we wanted to show appreciation. We could do that by sharing a drink, giving extra food, or any other thing that was extra and beyond," he said on the company's podcast. "When I was desperate for guests, I was so appreciative of every single guest that showed up. That experience cannot be replaced."

He's right. Aside from Andrew and his wife, Peggy, who joined him in the business in 1982, few, if any, of the company's employees know what it was like to have survived those humble beginnings. Today, employees prep ingredients each day, knowing there will be guests lining up to order plates of orange chicken, honey walnut shrimp, or beef and broccoli with a side of chow mein or fried rice.

Although employees may not realize its origins, they know that *giving* is a deeply held value that guides the company. It's a trait that Andrew believes begins with the individual. "I think giving back is a state of being. You're not calculating; you're giving of yourself," he said. To that end, the company has donated hundreds of millions of dollars to various charities, both out of its profits and from the practice of inviting guests to round up their bill for charity.

Deeply held values tend to go against conventional wisdom. It doesn't make business sense for a restaurant to give food away. That's exactly what makes this value unique for Panda Express. One of the easiest ways to uncover deeply held values is to ask questions like these:

- "What frustrates us the most in our organization?"
- "What are our greatest fears in the business?"
- "What really makes us angry when it happens?"

Fear and anger are often reactions against our values being challenged or violated. Look for the hidden values in your answers to these questions.

Values are the standards you live by. Ask *how*.

- How will you, as a company, always or never act?

- How will you, as an individual, always or never act?

- What are your permission-to-play values?

- What are your distinguishing values?

- What are your deeply held values?

Mission

A few years ago, I consulted with a multinational company in Houston that had been recently acquired by an investment group. With all the transition, the leadership wisely paused to evaluate every aspect of the business. The leadership team realized that, over the years, the company had taken on more product lines and various kinds of customers, and its varied offerings had stretched its resources and people too thin. To reach the vision they'd set their sights on for the next iteration of the business, the leadership team decided to narrow the company's focus.

We worked together to clarify the company's mission, asking questions about purpose, values, and long-term vision. Then, we looked at what they were currently doing and considered whether those things would move them toward their vision and help the company fulfill its purpose. With that clarity, they refined their mission by reducing the company's product line and focusing on a more specific customer profile. The process wasn't easy. Parts of the company that were no longer part of the mission were spun off and sold, which caused even more upheaval in the short term. The end result, however, was a much more focused and healthy company that has more than doubled its annual revenue, but more importantly, it has raised its equity value many times over.

Mission is the road you're moving along to get where you want to go. It's the tasks and effort you and your team members put in each day, and it requires focus.

Mission is the practical work you do. Ask *what*.

- What is the thing you do every day?

- What do you do to fulfill your purpose?

- What do you do to move toward your vision?

I want you to notice a few things. First, your values and purpose remain steady. While the road may turn and put you on a different mission, your values and purpose keep you from getting metaphorically stuck in a ditch on the side of the road. One of the interesting things about vision is that there can be multiple vision horizons ahead of you. You may have a life vision, a ten-year vision, an annual vision, or a vision for getting through each day. Part of leadership is understanding how much of your vision to cast to your team for them to join your mission journey.

Your culture ideology should create alignment. When you step back and look at the whole picture, you should be able to see that each piece works together toward the same end. Without this arrow, organizations naturally drift back toward chaos.

Vision

Vision is a picture of the future. It answers the question: If we are fulfilling the purpose while doing this mission, what could we accomplish?

I noted earlier that you can have multiple points on the horizon ahead of you. You might have long-range vision that looks thirty years into the future. You may also have a vision of what you want to achieve in the next thirty days. You need clarity about your vision so that you can align your mission and actually get to those points on the horizon. The multiplicity of horizons will inspire and guide the scale of the mission, something we will discuss in Part Four of this book.

Vision is a picture of the future. Ask *where*.

- Where are you going as a company?

- Where do you want to be five years from now? Ten years from now?

SMART(ER) Goals

SMARTER goals can be used to strategically plan for the journey ahead.

Specific—What do you want to accomplish?

Measurable—What metrics will help you mark progress toward that goal?

Achievable—Do you have the necessary skills and resources? If not, how will you acquire them?

Relevant—Is your goal aligned with your purpose and values? Will the goal help you reach the vision?

Time-Bound—What is the deadline for achieving the goal?

Evaluative—Is the goal in alignment with your values?

Rewarding—Does this goal energize you? Will achieving the goal provide a sense of achievement?

Culture Brand

Where does Culture Brand fit into this picture? Culture Brand is the engine (effort) that drives the vehicle (your mission) down that road you are traveling. It is the sum of everyone's efforts and attitudes. When you intentionally design and maintain your Culture Brand *engine*, it drives the organization forward on mission, operating at its highest efficiency, to attain the vision.

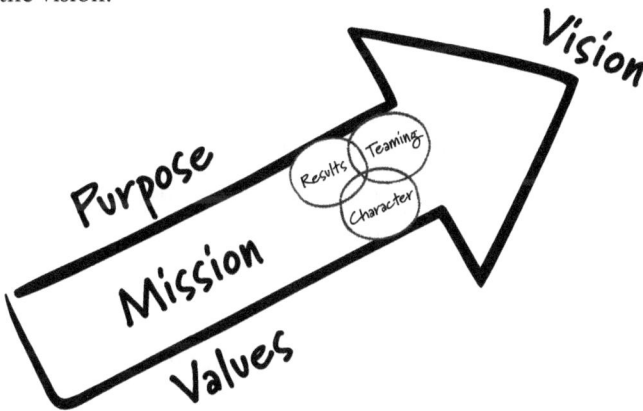

You are probably familiar with the sensation of driving a vehicle that is constantly pulling to one side because the wheels are out of alignment. Or maybe you've been on a trip with someone who insists on taking sightseeing detours that are "only a little out of the way." That extra work, friction, and distractions are what it feels like when culture is left to chance. Even with your core ideology—your PV²M—in place, the road is difficult.

Clarifying your PV²M is essential, but it is an incomplete solution. I'm sure you know of or have even worked at a company where the purpose, values, vision, and mission had been clearly identified and perhaps even posted conspicuously on the wall. I'm sure you've also noticed that most of the time, the daily operations look wildly different than what those noble-sounding words claim about the organization. When teams are unhealthy, it's often because there is a gap between core ideology and the organization's daily operations—not just the effort but the attitude.

Culture Brand

Culture Brand addresses the human element of business. It closes that gap with practical behavioral guidelines that keep everyone moving forward within the purpose, values, vision, and mission of the organization. In doing so, it ensures alignment and helps to minimize or even eliminate the resistance, friction, and detours that slow your progress or take you off track.

Speaking of tracks, as I wrote this chapter of the book, our family was watching the 2024 Olympic Games. We found so many of the events captivating, but running was especially riveting. I couldn't help but ponder the parallels of the PV²M of a track race. Purpose was represented by the event itself. The rules of the track represented values. The strategies each athlete employed to qualify for and hopefully win were their mission. And vision, of course, was the finish line. Culture was the experience and story of the athletes. Seen in the tenacity, determination, adversity, and passion of the athletes, culture brings color and emotion to the event. When all of these line up correctly, the convergence of purpose, values, vision, mission, *and* culture creates an amazing experience for everyone involved—from the spectators watching at home or in the stands to the event coordinators, reporters, coaches, and athletes themselves.

Culture Brand Makes PV²M Actionable

The Culture Brand methodology started to take shape when I shifted my attention to building healthy teams rather than focusing on fixing organizational dysfunction. I began to ask, *What are the positive behaviors we must have in an organization to have a high-performance culture?* Then, as I worked with leaders and teams around the country, one of the first things we did together was to make two lists—one of desired behaviors and one that highlighted the behaviors we wished would disappear forever. We started by writing words on sticky notes and posting them on the wall. These words represented the most necessary and most challenging behaviors that particular team encountered regularly.

With some time spent reflecting on and discussing these words, three behavior categories emerged. It was a theme I saw repeated with dozens of teams in various industries. I noticed, too, that other leaders and authors had identified a similar pattern. In his book, *The Ideal Team Player*, Pat Lencioni identified behavior categories that he labeled Hungry, Humble, and Smart. For several years, Chick-fil-A has relied on the categories of Competency, Chemistry, and Character to evaluate candidates. The prevalence of this pattern sparked more questions. I wondered . . .

What is the meta-theme behind all of these designs?

Are these constructs simply a summary of values?

What if each organization could have their own custom words that were unique to them?

What I determined was that the behavior categories always answered three questions:

1. How do **we** describe getting *results*?
2. How do **we** describe *teaming*?
3. How do **we** describe essential *character* traits?

Results, teaming, and character. These three essential elements shape Culture Brand—and the words that represent these categories are unique for every organization. Using this insight with my clients, we grouped their words into these three categories. I then asked them to identify three "umbrella" words that encompassed their unique way of describing these three essential cultural elements for their unique organizations.

The leadership teams I worked with loved the processes, and they appreciated that they now had a simple, measurable structure to measure behavior. They began challenging each other with these three words. Some teams used each word as a hashtag in their reports, and a sense of community and solidarity developed among them. It gave them a shortcut language for them to describe the culture they wanted. The leaders also noticed that no one was strong in all three areas—not even the leaders themselves. But everyone could grow in each area, and by combining their areas of strength, they were better together. That's the momentum Culture Brand creates.

Notice the question pondered about the correlation between these three words and values. Overlap certainly exists; in fact, some of our clients struggle initially to design their Culture Brand because they already have a set of clearly defined values. Sometimes, our clients have a catchy acronym that reflects their values. They are so attached to that expression of their values that it is hard for them to consider another approach. Occasionally, we discover that a company's existing values language is a perfect match for Culture Brand. When that's true, they incorporate that language into their Culture Brand design in a way that deepens the definitions and strengthens the impact of their values. Most of the time, however, our clients discover that values words are missing one or more of the key elements for success. Often, values reflect the personality of the founder or a few top leaders. The Culture Brand framework helps balance the essential elements for a healthy culture.

I am not advocating for the subversion or replacement of deeply held values. Keep them! Use them! Culture Brand makes them more meaningful by asking two powerful questions:

- How can you make those values measurable?
- How can you leverage those values in your people strategy?

Ultimately, the three words you land on to express your culture may show up in your purpose, values, vision, or mission—but they will sum them up in a way that's far more memorable and *actionable* than those cumbersome statements. And that's the point. Your Culture Brand takes your core ideology off the walls and attaches it to day-to-day behaviors and attitudes.

Purpose is *why* we do what we do; culture puts that *why* into motion.

Values are *how* we behave; culture makes values practical and applicable.

Mission is *what* we do; culture is *how* we do it.

Vision is *where* we want to go; culture makes the journey safe and meaningful for everyone.

You've heard of being purpose-driven, values-driven, vision-driven, or mission-driven. Culture Brand combines those ideas into one powerful concept and closes the gap between ideals and action, fueling *culture*-driven organizations. My goal is to give you a method of integrating and evaluating your team's success with your purpose, values, vision, and daily mission so they know *how* to win.

Culture Brand Is Scalable

The strong, successful leaders we work with seek to drive next-level growth, but these same leaders often face two challenging scenarios that make it difficult to stay true to the culture of the early days *and* scale the company:

1. The culture is difficult to scale consistently beyond the core leaders.
2. Their personal engagement in the business is limited and outpaced by an ever-expanding culture.

Over and over again, we see incredible leaders and business owners who put their heart and energy into creating a strong culture early when they were working shoulder to shoulder with their employees. As their businesses grew and they took on more responsibility, it became impossible to be everywhere at once. They used to know everyone in the company; now there are people working for them that they've never met. Without the leader's heart and passion driving it, the culture that helped the company grow got lost along the way.

These growth pains are not just felt by founders but also by various levels of leaders. An interesting and common paradox is that next-level leaders tend to be highly responsible people. The very trait that makes them great leaders can also keep them working harder rather than smarter in the business. Struggling under mounting responsibilities, they try to muscle through by themselves.

With Culture Brand, we help leaders multiply their efforts by equipping their emerging leaders to push the culture forward. Regardless of whether the company has grown to ten or two thousand, the concise and clear language of their Culture Brand captures their culture and makes it replicable.

So here we are. We are about to help you design your own Culture Brand. In the next section, I will unpack the elements of the Culture Brand and help you understand how it works for you and your team. After that, I will show you how to build your own custom Culture Brand and some first steps for implementing it into your routines.

Clarifying your PV²M is essential. Your core ideology lays the groundwork, but it is not enough. Culture Brand fills the gap between knowing and doing. Like a compass, it's the tool that equips everyone on the team—from top leadership to entry-level members—to stay aligned with the mission while navigating the obstacles along the way so that you can move with confidence toward the vision on the horizon *together*.

Call to Action: Clarify Your PV²M

Reflecting on your answers for your purpose, values, visions, and mission, consider the following questions:

- Do all the pieces move you in the same direction?

- What, if anything, is pulling you or your team members off course?

- Are you remaining true to purpose and values in the daily work that you do?

- Will your efforts take you where you want to go?

PART TWO:
LEADERS DESIGN CULTURE

Culture fails without results, teaming, and character.

When they'd met that first time at The Coffee Nook, Scott had explained his process for understanding what culture was, and most importantly, what it was for his company and his team. Kate appreciated his transparency.

"About three years ago, I was done," Scott told her. "I couldn't seem to make it work. My team was miserable, our guests were complaining, and I was ready to quit."

He had come back from the West Texas trip with a few ideas. He was committed to "tending the soil." He knew he needed to create that kind of workplace environment. What he didn't know was how to do that, and not knowing frustrated him. He had an MBA and years of experience in operations. But nothing had prepared him for the challenges of building and managing a healthy team—something he needed not just to keep the business afloat but to do it in a way that was sustainable for him and his family. He wanted to be a business owner, but he didn't want his life to be consumed by the business 24/7.

He had the desire to be a good leader. And he'd proven to his own detriment that he was willing to put in the time and effort. So what was he missing?

In an attempt to figure that out, Scott headed to the library and pulled every leadership book from the shelves and piled them on the table. The sheer number of books and the wide range of topics within leadership were daunting. He found titles focused on goal-setting, conflict management, vision-casting, accountability, ownership, attitude, time-management, developing others, and so many more. Even more daunting was the prospect of studying and mastering so many subjects. That would take years. And he didn't have that kind of time.

Hours later, he wasn't enlightened so much as overwhelmed—until a pattern emerged. He walked over and started sorting the books onto three tables. He stepped back and wrote three words on a scrap of paper and boxed them in: results, teaming, character.

Taking a moment to consider everything those categories represented, he felt as if he had just deciphered the Rosetta Stone. Every promising leadership idea fit one—or more—of those three.

He sketched arrows between them and wrote: *Culture fails without results, teaming, and character.*

results ⟶ teaming ⟶ character

Culture fails without results, teaming, and character.

No wonder there was so much miscommunication on his team. They were essentially speaking different languages! Some of his team members were task oriented and often tuned out everyone around them. And he was convinced that some of his employees showed up at work solely for the social interaction. Those were often the ones who never seemed to get their work done.

Emotions and frustration levels ran high as those who were more relational felt run over by those who were task focused. On the flipside, those who were just trying to get their work done were often irritated by their more chatty coworkers.

Culture fails without results, teaming, and character.

Thinking about the difference in his employees, he drew a ladder. He labeled the right side Hard Skills and listed things related to technical experience and expertise: certifications, output, sales, and consistency. The left side, he labeled People Skills. On that side, he listed behaviors that spoke more to emotional intelligence: humility, self-awareness, communication, and collaboration.

Looking at the ladder he'd sketched, he thought about the people who worked for him. Most struggles on his team weren't due to capability; they were about the behaviors on the left side—their willingness to work with others, receive feedback, own mistakes, and their trustworthiness.

Beneath the ladder, he wrote: *Leaders must develop both sides—or people fall off the ladder.*

The more he thought about it, the more convinced he became that if he could help his team agree on a way to get results, work together, and show up with a strong personal character, he could get everyone together and moving in the same direction.

Could it really be that simple? he wondered.

He had to find out.

Determined to make the coffee shop a success, Scott scheduled an after-hours meeting for the following Monday. He made attendance mandatory—but the time would be paid, and he was bringing in dinner for the entire team.

That Monday evening after closing, Scott pushed a few tables together and set out some markers and sticky notes. He set up two whiteboards on easels and wrote Good Teams on one and Bad Teams on another.

After everyone had filled their plates and found a seat, Scott said, "I know we've had some issues lately, but I feel like we can turn some things around. To get started, I want you to be honest about what's important to you. What would make this a really great place to work?"

Culture Brand

Darrin piped up immediately. "You give us all the free food we want! And double pay on Saturday!"

A couple people chuckled. Maria rolled her eyes. Scott managed to keep his expression neutral but considered whether this meeting might be a waste of time and money. He remembered Clark's attitude toward him after his tractor mistake and chose to keep things light.

Scott smiled good-naturedly. "Alright, sure. But here in the real world, what makes a great work environment? What kind of people do you want to work with?"

"People I can count on," Maria said.

"Yes, good! Can you put that in just a word or two?" Scott asked.

"Trustworthy. Kind?"

"Yes!" Scott pointed to the pad of sticky notes in front of her. "Write those down and put them on the board."

"People who care about doing a good job." The response came from the oldest of the bunch, Max. He was a retired teacher and was great with customers. He was also meticulous in his work—which meant it took him longer than anyone else to finish a task. But he always got it done. Eventually.

"Absolutely. Caring. Write it down, Max!"

And so it went. The team listed good and bad qualities. When the boards were covered with sticky notes, they sorted the words into the three categories of results, teamwork, and character.

After they'd sorted all the words, Scott asked, "What words would sum up the things in each of these categories?" He was looking for a mantra of sorts—a rally cry that could help them remember what they all agreed was important to them. "And just for fun, let's keep it coffee focused."

His team really got into the brainstorming exercise, tossing out ideas. Some were ridiculous, and some were thoughtful. Before the night was out, they'd landed on Grind, Brew, Savor. *Grind* had a double meaning to remind them that getting results required toughness and grit but also exactness and excellence. *Brew* was about teamwork. You needed all the right elements—water, heat, beans, reliable equipment—to make a great cup of coffee. And *Savor* related to character, the traits that made others want to work with you.

As Kate thought about what Scott had referred to as his "library epiphany," she asked herself the same question: *Could it be that simple?*

After doing her own deep dive into leadership topics, she came to the same conclusion. It was an amazingly simple and straightforward view of leadership: results, teaming, and character.

Those three key ideas provided a framework—a way to identify needs (what was working and what wasn't) and to measure progress toward improvement.

Looking at leadership through the lens of results, teaming, and character gave Kate a way to better understand her leadership team and how to maximize their strengths and encourage them to improve in their growth areas. She felt certain it would do the same for them and their teams.

"It seems that character fits in both teaming and results, doesn't it?" The question had come from one of Kate's VPs that day in the conference room.

Scott hadn't missed a beat. "I thought so, too, at first. The way we work and how we treat people do seem like character qualities. And they are. But I couldn't get around the fact that there was something special about the topics of the books I'd sorted onto the character table. We all want—no, we *need*—our people to have high-quality character, to be dependable and coachable and to take ownership of their work. Character colors the other two aspects of teaming and results, for good and for bad. If someone isn't getting the job done well or on time but is coachable, they are more likely to improve their skills and results because they're open to taking and acting on feedback. But if they're high on execution and somewhat influential but low on dependability, ownership, or coachability, they can be divisive. Developing their character can help those people become even stronger as leaders in your organization."

And if they aren't open to improvement, they have the potential to derail everything, Kate thought with a few specific people in mind.

"Oh, good, it's arts-and-crafts time," Ryan said when Kate handed out stacks of sticky notes and markers to her leaders.

Ignoring the sarcasm, Kate thanked them for taking the time away from the office and their families for the retreat. "I know you all know there are some things that aren't working. So let's figure out what that is—and figure out what to do about it." She tapped her computer and projected the mission and vision statement on a large screen that hung at one end of the room.

"I believe in this mission. I believe that if we work toward this mission—together and consistently—we will be able to achieve all of our goals as an organization. But what I've noticed is that we don't seem to be in agreement about how to live out this mission and move toward our vision."

She paused and looked around the room. She'd purposely chosen a space that was more comfortable and inviting than the conference room at their office. The executives had left their suits at home and wore jeans and shoes that were more suitable for golf than a business meeting. They looked back at her from comfortable armchairs and couches. And as was typical, she saw a mix of expressions and engagement.

"There are behaviors in our organization that help us and some that hurt us on the path to winning at our mission." She pointed to a blank wall adjacent to the projector screen where she'd posted two signs. One read Good Teams and the other, Bad Teams. "I want us to fill that wall with every characteristic we can think of to describe good teams and bad teams. The words don't have to be about this team but any team you've ever been part of or watched. You have ten minutes, and I want everyone to put at least fifteen characteristics on the wall."

A few of her leaders jumped right in, jotting down words and walking over to the wall to post them under the proper label. Slowly, everyone joined in. When the timer rang, Kate smiled.

"Nice! This is a great start. Now, let's take another ten minutes, and without repeating what is already on the wall, add ten more qualities for leaders. What are five good qualities and five additional bad qualities of leaders?"

When the time was up, they worked to find a positive word that was the opposite of any of the negative qualities listed.

Then they sorted all of the qualities into three categories: results, teaming, and character. As the hour drew to a close, Kate pointed to mission and vision statements that were still on the screen and said, "If this is what's important to us," she swiveled to point at the words they had collected and sorted, "we have to live out and live up to these good qualities."

So far, so good. The exercise had created a lot of interaction—and a few tiffs as they identified some of the negative qualities that were far too evident amongst some on the team. Overall, though, it had been a positive experience.

"When we come back from the break, I want us to find the words that pull these qualities into focus and succinctly express who we are, or at least who we want to become as a company, and how we will work going forward. Three words, one for each category, to encapsulate what we want our culture to be."

Culture Brand

As her leaders mingled, she overheard a few of them already brainstorming ideas. Not everyone, of course—a few remained skeptical. She shrugged and decided to focus on those who were engaged.

Time would tell who could live into the culture they were creating—and who couldn't.

Chapter 4
Creating a *Winning* Culture

*Give me a lever long enough and a fulcrum on
which to place it, and I shall move the world.*
—Archimedes

I took woodshop class in the sixth grade, and my first project was a three-legged stool. It was a challenging project, and while I didn't make the most beautiful stool, I completed the task successfully. It wasn't until years later that I realized why the teacher had insisted on a three-legged stool. Building a four-legged stool would have taken more time, but more significantly, it would have been much harder to get it balanced. Any variance in the length of its legs would have made it wobble. Even if the legs were perfect, if the floor was slightly uneven, a four-legged stool would wobble.

The shop teacher chose a three-legged stool for the project attempt because, even with slight imperfections that were bound to occur with our first attempts at woodworking, the final product would be able to stand on its own.

Three-legged stools are always stable. The three legs provide balance and strength. And for a shop class full of eleven- and twelve-year-olds, the goal of creating something we could actually use was attainable and winnable.

What I want for you and your organization is a culture that offers the kind of strength and balance that provides stability and puts winning within reach for everyone on the team. For that to occur, you need alignment within and throughout your organization.

In the previous chapter, I explained how our work to help create healthy teams revealed a pattern of three categories of behaviors: results, teaming, and character. Good or bad, it's the convergence of results, teaming, and character that provides a picture of a company's culture. The more we looked at behavior through these three lenses, the more clearly we could see that winning teams know what it looks like to be strong in each of these areas. Healthy teams can answer these critical questions:

1. How do **we** describe getting **results**?
2. How do **we** describe **teaming**?
3. How do **we** describe essential individual **character** traits?

Let's take a closer look at each element of a winning culture.

Results

Regardless of what kind of business you're in, results are required. For our clients in the quick-service food industry, the top priority results are profit, food safety, quality, and customer experience. With various levels of responsibility in the structure of the organization, each level will impact the top result areas in different ways. Thinking back to the ladder example, we would still expect the same attitude about results at every level in the organization, but with varying degrees of impact and responsibility. Breaking these down into tangible and winnable behaviors is part of having a strong Culture Brand. What "results" behavior do we expect from the newest entry-level team member and the top operations director? Customers expect a clean and safe environment. The tasks required of a team member might be bathroom checks and managing spills, while the director may manage vendors for pest control and driveway maintenance. In the process, they will both be expected to keep a strong results-oriented culture in the roles they have.

Although results look different at every level of our organizations, they are nonnegotiable. To accomplish the mission, the team must deliver results—and every team member must do their part. Without results, the mission fails. If we over-index on results, however, and miss the next two components, the victories will be hollow, and the environment will feel toxic.

These are benefits of a results culture:

- The team knows how to win.
- It provides focus on where you are going.
- Accountability is high without apology or excuse.
- Quality is elevated instead of ignored.
- It helps a team know when to push for more and when to recover.
- It is usually the easiest of the three to measure and enforce.

Teaming

People are the most valuable resource of any organization. Everything works better when people work together. That's teaming, and it's where synergy and momentum happen. I use the verb *teaming* to emphasize that it is not just a category, it is an activity. *Teaming* is the multiplying factor for getting work done.

When teamwork is low, we have a room full of individual contributors where everyone is working for themselves. But when we put a team-minded person in leadership, engagement goes up. People feel cared for and included in the shared mission. The daily work feels more meaningful because it points more to what we are doing together. Resources are shared, and knowledge is transferred instead of siloed.

The benefits of a team working together are powerful:

- Collaboration and synergy lead to three times (or greater) return on effort.
- Community and unity foster a psychologically safe environment.
- Emotional connection builds a sense of trust and loyalty.
- Higher engagement keeps the mission moving forward.
- People feel a greater sense of purpose in their work, which helps to reduce attrition.

Character

The word *character* in this context speaks to a team member's ownership, coachability, and dependability. Each of these qualities have impact on results and relationships, but they stand squarely in the personal character bucket.

- **Ownership** is about taking personal responsibility and care for the organization's mission.
- **Coachability** requires that the team member receive feedback and be willing and eager to grow.
- **Dependability** ensures that team members can count on one another. A dependable team member shows up with the right attitude and puts in their best effort every day.

A person's character acts as a governor for the rest of their behavior, which makes character the single most important of the three aspects of winning culture. It is also the hardest one to change because it is far more challenging to change hearts than to change minds. If someone is coachable, dependable, and willing to take ownership of themselves and their work, very often, you can train them in the skills they need to succeed.

Character opens the door for true self-leadership. Take a moment to think about your personal character as it relates to your leadership. How would you rate yourself in each of the areas of ownership, coachability, and dependability?

Whatever your mission is, it cannot successfully be accomplished without all three of these essentials—results, teaming, and character—from everyone. A winning culture calls each person on the team to be strong—or at least willing to grow—in every area.

You Need All Three

Consistent success and customer satisfaction cannot be maintained without all three of these areas.

- Attention to *results* is required for accurate, fast, and excellent product delivery.
- *Teaming* is essential for coordinating all the moving parts of a top-level drive-thru or an efficient and clean dining experience.
- The right *character* of each team member is necessary to ensure a pleasant experience and an enjoyable work environment.

If the team or its individual members lack these critical elements, the experience is lost. Customer satisfaction tanks. Team member engagement drops. Hiring becomes a growing challenge. It takes the convergence of all three areas for the mission of serving guests with quality and care to be accomplished.

Pause here to consider this point. Once you see it, you can't unsee it. A winning culture requires results, teaming, *and* character. Consider what it looks like when one or more of these three elements are missing and how it affects the organization.

High Results, High Character, Low Teaming

Individuals who rank high in results and character but low in teaming are undeniably productive. They get stuff done, but it's often with little regard for the people around them. These people will do their work and typically outperform the others—except when it comes to dealing with people. When it comes to their team members, they are less likely to share their experience or training because they want to be the ones who win. They don't see a need to get to know or engage with the customer. Their attitude toward people has a negative impact on the customer experience, so they aren't likely to bring in repeat customers. Most of the team will struggle to grow and engage around this person.

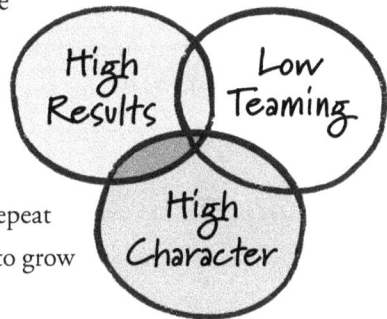

High
Results

Low
Teaming

High
Character

High Team, High Character, Low Results

If you have people who are high in team and character but low in results, they may create a warm, engaging environment, but you may wish they would set goals and care more about quality. This person interfaces well with the rest of the team and customers, but they don't pay attention to details. They tend to be distracted by conversations and may spend more time talking than getting their work done. They might be disorganized but apologetic. They will forget to upsell the customer, and they may not try to hit their bonus. They will be liked by customers and team members, but they struggle to build consistent wins for the organization.

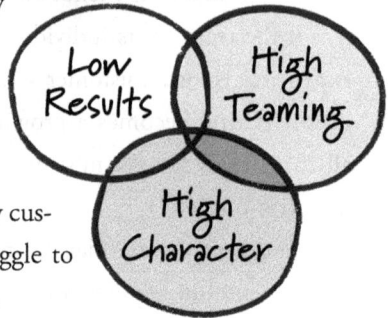

High Results, High Team, Low Character

If you have someone who is high in team and results but low in character, they will struggle with dependability or ownership. They will probably not be very coachable because, in their eyes, they never do anything wrong— someone else is always to blame for their mistakes or sloppy work. At its extreme, these low-character team members tend to cause division. They misuse their influence with a few loyal friends at work, but most people avoid them because they are cliquish. They use any influence they may have for their own gain.

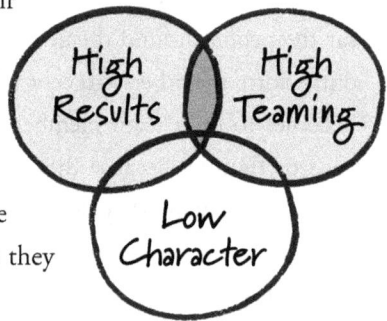

Results Focused Only

Results-focused people often come across as too direct, pushy, or harsh because they appear to care only about the bottom line. Sometimes, results-oriented leaders allow the win to overshadow the journey and may be so focused on the task that they run people over on their way to the finish

Creating a *Winning* Culture

line. But let's be honest: If we want to get work done, we turn to them for action. We need results. We get benefits from results-driven people. They are focused, goal-oriented, task-driven, solutions-minded, and direct.

Teaming Focused Only

The teaming-only person tends to be the charming person who gets away with too much. They are influential, but since they are low in results and character behaviors, there is low trust in them on tasks and ownership. They tend to rely on their ability to blend in with the team without taking responsibility for errors and goals.

Character Only

The character-only person tends to be the nice, quiet person we can't seem to find a good place for in the business. They are often shuffled from one team to another. They may even receive feedback well, but it doesn't get put into action. They have little influence among their teammates, and they struggle to drive for results. We keep them because they are nice and amiable, but they are not moving the team or the business forward. They are less than an individual contributor because someone has to guide them constantly.

My guess is that as you read these descriptions, the names of people in your organization came to mind. Chances are good that at least a few of those names belong to people who have been recently exited. Remember the ladder of development from Chapter One? People don't typically exit the organization from the right side of the ladder (skills and tenure). They typically exit or are exited because of behavioral issues related to personality conflicts and emotional intelligence.

The point of identifying what results, teaming, and character look like for your organization is not to start diagnosing and dismissing everyone who fails to meet all three areas. The point is to discover what everyone needs to aim for to get there and to help each person get there.

95

When you know what a winning culture looks like—and what it requires from each person—you have clear standards you can use to hire, coach, promote, and exit people. I coach my client organizations to look to hire people who are fairly strong in two areas and growing in a third. If you are looking to add or promote a leader in your organization, and the candidate you're considering has serious struggles in two of these areas, they are probably not the best choice. They have too much to overcome in the time that you need. But if they have some strength in two areas and they are moldable and eager to learn in the third, that's a win. Promote them, or get them in your organization! (Later, I'll share a few strategies you can use to coach the leaders on your team who have gaps in any of these critical areas.)

What about you? The examples given above are intentionally extreme. I hope you will see, however, that you probably have at least one area that is glaringly lower than the other two. This is to be expected. A Culture Brand is not designed to create perfection. It is designed to identify our strengths and weaknesses so we can create strategies for growth and compensations for our gaps. We are all uniquely designed and view our environment through those unique lenses. Culture Brand is a kind of corrective lens to help us all get a full view of the environment we desire to create.

Leveraging Strengths to Lead Culture

Alex Honnold is a rock climber known for scaling incredible heights. Not long ago, I watched the biopic about his life, *Free Solo*, with my hands covering my eyes. Peeking between my fingers as he scaled Yosemite's El Capitan without a rope, I noticed that for every move, Honnold establishes as many holds as possible before reaching for a new hold. The same principle can be applied to leading a winning culture.

Culture Brand is built on results, teaming, and ownership, but the reality is that it is rare for anyone—even leaders—to be naturally strong in all three areas. Personally, I know I am strong in the team and character areas and that I can struggle in the results category. My tendency is to choose people over results. Awareness is the beginning of transformation. Being a culture leader requires us to be aware of both our areas of strength and the places where we need to grow. With Culture Brand, you learn to leverage your areas of strength to grow in the third area. If I am a strong team player and have been taking personal ownership, I am more likely to grow because I can use those strengths to support my growth in a results area. We can

> **Awareness is the beginning of transformation.**

use our strength areas as an anchor point when stretching for a new area of growth. We leverage our strengths to overcome our weaknesses—not to just accept and ignore them.

When you are making a big reach, start from a place of strength in the other areas. Honnold's mission was to scale that massive wall of granite. Our mission may not be life-and-death, but we can still leverage each move to inch our way toward completion of the goal. When those moves are defined and supported by a winning culture, they allow us to close the gap between where we are and where we want to be.

> What are your two areas of greatest strength? What are you reaching for? How can you leverage your strengths to reach for that third area?

How Culture Leaders Leverage Results: Laser Focus

Like a laser, a goal-oriented leader brings focus to the mission. Focus is what makes lasers so powerful. By gathering light that would otherwise go unnoticed and pointing in a single, narrow direction, a laser produces the kind of power that can blast through steel, engrave diamonds, or create intricate designs. The fascinating thing about lasers is that the light is everywhere, but it's the focus that makes it so productive.

When leaders focus on the mission, they direct their efforts and those of the team toward the goal.

How Culture Leaders Leverage Teaming: Force Multiplier

While results provide focus, teaming maximizes everyone's efforts. Leaders who are effective at teaming know that this aspect of culture is about more than building strong relationships. While relationship and creating a sense of belonging are crucial, leaders leverage teaming by being intentional about developing other people. They share knowledge, inspire collaborative planning, and encourage others to grow. When a dependable, results-oriented leader learns to collaborate and develop others, they can double, triple, or quadruple their efforts. Teaming is a force multiplier!

How Culture Leaders Leverage Character: Transformation Point

Character is the hinge point for Culture Brand. Most leaders find that their workforce is somewhat divided between results-focused and relationship-focused people. When we conduct personality profiles for teams, the separation between these two groups is often stark. A few people ride the line between results and relationships, but when circumstances force them to choose, their behavior will side with one or the other.

It is character that allows people to grow in their weaker areas. Let me give an example: Let's say you are a highly relational person and can influence a small or large group of people, but you struggle to hold others accountable. The only way to grow in holding others accountable is through being coachable, dependable, and taking ownership. You leverage your care for people to go deeper in your self-leadership to grow in your results behavior.

The opposite is also true. Let's say you are a driven and direct leader who is goal-oriented, but your team members are afraid to make suggestions and tend to hide problems from you because they fear your reaction. The only way for you to improve as a relational leader is to be coachable, take ownership of your actions, and show that you can be dependable with new behavior for being collaborative and encouraging.

Self-leadership through personal character behaviors is the path to success on both sides of the results–relationships continuum. This truth is why so many successful organizations follow the practice of hiring for character and training for skill.

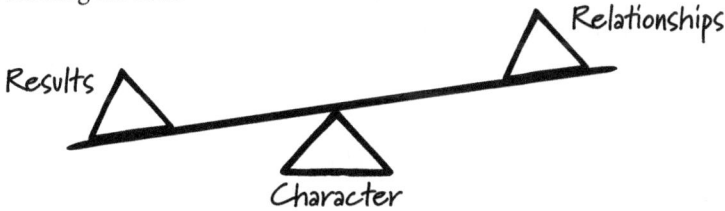

The ancient Greek philosopher and mathematician Archimedes said, "Give me a lever long enough and a fulcrum on which to place it, and I shall move the world." Character may not be the lever, but I believe it is the fulcrum. Think of it this way: If I leverage my ability to invest in people against the fulcrum of being coachable and taking ownership, I can shift my capacity to get results. If I am stronger in results and press that strength against a steadfast personal humility, I can grow in my ability to influence and multiply effort through others.

If you're not quite convinced, then remove the fulcrum from leverage. I could have enormous strength in either getting results or building relationships, and if I don't have a coachable, dependable character with a willingness to take personal ownership, I will not get very far. The path to growth is *through* character. Coachable and dependable character takes ownership of their actions.

Leading Culture with Clarity

The three-legged stool of results, teaming, and character makes it easy for your team to see how they are expected to interact with the people around them and whether they are contributing to the forward motion of the mission. What was invisible or intangible now has context and actionable behavior attached to it. Culture design, however, can't stop here. These three main categories are like huge buckets that hold the entire world of leadership thought. And words, remember, hold different meanings to different people. To make Culture Brand most effective, take it deeper by packing powerful and precise meaning into each word.

As we worked with clients to identify the three words that represented what results, teaming, and character meant to them, we collected so much great information about what each team wanted for their organizations. Before we removed all those sticky notes from the wall, our clients often pulled a few words that expanded the definitions of each of the three main areas. Some teams kept four or five words to help them explain in more practical ways what each of the three words that comprised their new Culture Brand meant.

After doing this sticky-note exercise with new clients for a couple of years, we noticed that the clarifying words our clients saved also followed a pattern. For each of the three main categories (results, teaming, and character), three subcategories became apparent.

Results

- Goal-driven: sets clear and measurable targets and gives them priority ahead of other important or distracting tasks.
- Pursues Excellence: views perfection as a moving target and seeks to be constantly moving toward the highest quality. They compete against the last result or the biggest obstacle.
- Holds Others Accountable: measures results against action and enforces established standards when dealing with people.

Teaming

- Collaborates: creates multiple levels of communication and clarity in every direction. They share and invite information, progress, challenges, and ideas.
- Develops Others: invests in others without restraint and share their library of knowledge willingly.
- Encourages: looks for positive ways to energize others and seek to see the best in those around them.

Character

- Coachable: handles feedback with maturity and look for ways to grow. They actively seek truth and are hungry to improve.
- Dependable: reliable in their attitude and commitments.
- Takes Ownership: doesn't make excuses, and they take responsibility for their work, behavior, and influence.

Regardless of whether our organizations adopted these exact words or found a unique way to express these subcategories, the concepts were consistent. Each of these nine subcategories brings more depth and shape to an organization's Culture Brand. The clarity offers a quick, comprehensive view of culture behaviors that team members can immediately understand and implement as a guide to move the mission forward.

As our clients designed their Culture Brand, they formed their people strategy around these simple targets. The clarity helped to eliminate frustrations and accelerate development with their people. Accountability cascaded from the core team to the front of their organizations. The Culture Brand effect was transformational. Engagement climbed, and leaders grew in confidence because they knew how to coach their team members.

The transparency allowed everyone to see where growth and support were needed most. Trust accelerated, and community abounded. If a leader admitted that they weren't great at holding others accountable, a peer would respond, "Neither am I; let's find a way to grow in that area." Or someone who was strong in that area might respond, "It's not a problem for me. I'd be willing to hold you accountable about holding others accountable." Open conversations like this became common as teams shifted to a growth-mindset.

Lead Out Loud

Some people argue that *culture is caught, not taught.* Can your team members observe your behavior and understand your culture? Perhaps, to a degree. But relying on your team members or leaders to just "get" your culture is risky. Yes, modeling is powerful and important, but as a culture leader, you now know that leaving culture to chance leads to chaos.

One of our LeadersQ executive coaches, Danette High, came up with the phrase "leading out loud" to describe what it takes to ensure that Culture Brand permeates the organization. Leading out loud involves modeling desired behavior, certainly, but it takes people development a step further by openly and consistently explaining what you do—and why.

Leadership shouldn't be mystical or hidden. Leadership should be done out loud. If you want to develop new leaders and stronger leaders, equip people with tools and understanding by talking about the tools, methods, and resources you use so they can learn to use them as well. This principle works with any book you are reading or podcast you hear. If you learn something new, share the tool as you implement it. The main goal of leading out loud is to make leadership reproducible. If we can demystify our methods, others can imitate our models.

Culture Brand is a way to lead out loud. It is designed to be openly used and repeatedly implemented. As you talk about how you're building the culture and explain how the behaviors you're modeling support the culture, you teach them to adopt and share the same behaviors. Leading out loud moves you *together* toward accomplishing the mission that helps you reach your shared vision.

Leading Culture Transformation with Story

Stories are a powerful and simple way to immediately engage people with your PV²M and Culture Brand. By illustrating your Culture Brand in action, stories spark people's imagination. Curating and sharing stories is part of leading out loud. You can highlight instances where you've seen or heard about people showing up in positive ways, fulfilling what it means to succeed in results, teaming, or character. Pay attention and catch people exemplifying desired behaviors.

If the idea of becoming a storyteller makes you nervous, keep in mind that stories don't need to be long or complicated to be powerful. What you're looking for are two-minute stories that you can share about your team that are relevant to your Culture Brand.

Let's say you chose the word *respect* for teaming. While you're talking with someone on your team, you learn that one of your team members visited another in the hospital. That's respect! When you share the story and highlight the act of kindness of a team member going out of their way to show care for and encourage another, mention how that represents the organization's desire to show respect for one another. Simple. Become a story curator for your organization and start celebrating the kind of behavior that you want to see more of.

Call to Action: Create Stories

Gather ideas for three stories from your organization. Find a results story, a teaming story, and a character story. Share those stories and their connection to your team's selected Culture Brand words in your next team meeting.

Stories have shaped cultures for millennia. One easy way to craft a story is to follow the STAR method.

Situation: What were the beginning circumstances? Choose your time, one person, and the location.

Trouble: What was the desire, and what was the problem?

Action: What step did the person take that changed the situation?

Result: What finally happened, and what was the impact?

Conclude your story with the impact message and relate it to one of the three areas: getting results, teaming together, or personal character.

For more tips for story crafting, check out *Story Dash* by David Hutchens.

How is that our culture?

Before the end of the leadership retreat, the team had landed on the words *Advance*, *Elevate*, and *Trust* to define the culture they wanted. And as her people started to live out the qualities those words expressed, Kate noticed a change. In their weekly meetings, the conference room buzzed with a different kind of energy. The silent stares and crossed arms that had once put her on guard during meetings were, for the most part, things of the past. And for the first time in months, people were talking *to* one another rather than *at* one another.

As the quarter drew to a close, the numbers were positive all the way around. And when sales hit a record high the following quarter, she took it as evidence that the culture changes had taken root.

Production finally operated on schedule, and customer service complaints had dropped. Kate's reports for the board were getting easier to write—and easier to deliver.

She should have been thrilled. And she was . . . mostly.

The progress had come from a thousand tiny course corrections—feedback loops, cross-functional check-ins, new accountability meetings. Even Ryan, her most vocal skeptic, had begun using the phrase "our team" more than "my team." The words mattered. So did the shift behind them.

Culture Brand

Kate stood at the window of her office late one afternoon as the sun began to set. She smiled at the thought of how far they'd come. Maybe Scott's "soil" metaphor was working after all.

The next morning, Kate walked into the end-of-quarter meeting with coffee in hand and a rare sense of optimism. She regularly met with her executive team, and she'd heard a lot in the past few months about the improvements that had been made within the departments. But this was the first time to meet with the department leaders and managers since they'd launched the culture transformation initiative with Advance, Elevate, Trust.

She looked out at the directors and managers who filled the Gateway—the largest meeting space in the building. These were the people who were driving the culture changes from within, and she was grateful for their buy-in. "Before we dive into the numbers," she said, "I just want to say thank you. We're trending in the right direction, and that's because of you."

Laughter rippled through the room when someone quipped, "You mean we finally got something right?"

Even Kate laughed. "Yes, finally."

They reviewed metrics and project updates—mostly positive.

As she was closing the meeting, Alex, one of the sales team's most dependable managers, raised his hand.

"Can I ask something?" His tone was hesitant.

"Of course," Kate said.

Alex stood and cleared his throat. He didn't look around the room but kept his focus on Kate. "We've done a lot of work this year to define who we are—our values, our mission, our culture. But yesterday I overheard a director telling her team to skip the customer follow-up calls so they could 'hit the numbers.'" He paused. "We say this is our culture . . . but how is *that* our culture?"

The room went quiet.

How is that our culture?

Kate felt the sting of the question. She wanted to defend the progress they'd made—but she couldn't ignore the truth in his words.

He wasn't criticizing; he was holding them accountable.

"That's a fair question, Alex." She spotted Ben, the VP of Sales, sitting next to Alex's direct supervisor. The woman's bright red face told Kate exactly who had encouraged her team to skip the follow-up calls. *Is that anger or embarrassment?* Kate wondered. "We've worked hard to change what we do. Maybe it's time to look closer at how we're doing it."

Heads around the room nodded in agreement. Alex's supervisor stared straight ahead, avoiding eye contact. Ben, however, didn't look away when she caught his attention. Instead, he gave her a thoughtful look, tipping his head ever so slightly in acknowledgment.

That night, Kate couldn't shake the conversation. She replayed Alex's words again and again. *How is that our culture?*

They had systems, goals, and results—but maybe not alignment.

Her phone buzzed—a text from Scott:

How's the team doing?

> Better. But I think we've been chasing results without realizing we're off course.

Sounds like it's time for an alignment check.

She realized this next phase wasn't about building something new—it was about staying straight when the days were long and distractions tempting.

The following week, during the executive team meeting, she said, "We've come a long way, but I need to address what Alex brought up last week." She kept her tone direct and calm. "Our culture— Advance, Elevate, Trust—isn't just something we say. It's something we do. And I know it's tempting to let the urgency for results take precedence over everything else. If we're going to win long term, however, we have to remember what we stand for."

She paused, then added, "If our behaviors don't match our beliefs, then all the work we've put in over the past several months will be for nothing—the results won't last if we fall back into the old habits that take us off course."

Relief set in when she saw understanding in their eyes, not compliance but *conviction*.

Driving home that evening, Kate felt the tension ease. Their culture had created a healthy level accountability, and they were growing—not just as a company but as people. Still, she sensed another challenge coming. Growth always exposed what needed pruning next.

Chapter 5
Customizing YOUR Winning Culture

A hallmark of a healthy creative culture is that its people feel free to share ideas, opinions, and criticisms.
—Ed Catmull

I don't live too far from the old Chisholm Trail, the famous 800-mile route that was once used to drive cattle from South Texas to Kansas, where the cattle were sold or shipped farther north by train. Between about 1867 and 1884, an estimated five million head of cattle made the trek north, and every one of them had a brand to identify its owner. Ranchers' livestock brands, like Richard H. Chisholm's H C Bar and Captain Richard King's Running W (which is still used today and is the logo for Ford's King Ranch edition trucks), were recognizable from Texas to Kansas and probably beyond. The brand protected the ranchers' interests because people knew who and what those brands represented.

The same should be true today of an organization's brands, although today a brand is about far more than property ownership.

Brand reflects the emotional connection people have with your product or service. A strong positive brand is the result of a healthy culture that delivers on its mission. Spoken or implied, a brand carries the promise that the reputation earned by countless stories and encounters will remain consistent. Once a brand is accepted, there is an expectation that the values it represents will be honored and kept. Society is adept at noticing discrepancies, which means your brand must have absolute congruence in every respect:

1. What you say
2. What you do
3. How you look

Culture is an identity that takes precedence over any individual personality, opinion, or agenda. It comprises a sense of community, a common language, and expectations for behavior.

Culture Brand bridges these concepts. You've already seen the simplicity of this framework. Any organization can use it to connect the daily behaviors of the team to the mission that delivers the desired experience for everyone involved.

The power of this framework, however, comes from customizing it for your organization and your PV²M. Recognizable brands are not generic. Neither are unifying, compelling cultures bland or exactly like anyone else. In this chapter, you'll move from concept to application by designing *your* unique Culture Brand.

Step One: Gather Your Leaders

Every organization needs to have rhythms for meetings throughout the year. One of those annual rhythms should be setting aside a time to examine the business from the highest perspective and look as far into the future as possible. This type of meeting is ideal for introducing Culture Brand. Alternatively, set aside some time for everyone to gather and focus on specific mission-centering, culture-defining moments. Lay the groundwork by reviewing or sharpening your PV²M, then use the following steps to discover your unique Culture Brand.

Step Two: Good and Bad Team Traits

Hand out sticky-note pads and markers that write boldly enough to be seen from a distance when the note is posted on the wall. Divide your leaders into small teams or pairs and challenge them to identify as many good and bad team behaviors as possible. Set a goal for each group to identify ten to fifteen behaviors or traits for each category: results, teaming, and character. More is better.

Make it clear that these qualities can come from any source, present or past, and they don't necessarily have be from a work setting. Some ideas might come from their experience on sports teams or working with community organizations or clubs.

Then, have them post their sticky notes on the wall under labels marked Results, Teaming, and Character.

When I do this exercise with a leadership team, I remind participants that all of the behaviors are character traits, but the character category is specifically related to traits pertaining to self-leadership. Words like *driven* or *collaborative* are both character traits, but they belong in the results and teaming categories, respectively. Words like *ownership* and *responsibility* go in the *character* category.

To avoid having everything end up under character, you might ask your leaders to identify the words that fit in the results or teaming sections first.

Step Three: Good and Bad Leader Traits

Repeat the process with a focus on leaders. Ask participants to identify traits or behaviors of great leaders and poor leaders. Encourage them to refrain from adding bad qualities by simply adding *not* to a word. It's better to use specific negative traits, rather than opposites of the positives, because these words can help you discover positive behaviors that might have been overlooked. (More on that in the next step.)

As before, have participants sort their words on the wall into the three categories. You may need to assist them and make sure they are being sorted well.

Step Four: Convert the Negatives to Positives

Next, get everyone involved at the wall with markers and new sticky notes. Ask your leaders to find all the negative words and write a powerful positive word to overcome them.

Why are we doing negatives? Negatives can help you identify what frustrates you most *and* matters most to you. Here's a simple example of a negative shining a light on your values: You notice that at least one person is always slightly late to every meeting. Some people may not be bothered by that, but you are. As you dig into this irritation, you can begin to ask what value is being challenged for you. If it truly irritates you, it could be challenging your value for respect. Another person might say it is inefficient. A third person may say it challenges their control of the room. Find the root value, and you have discovered a very important aspect to consider for your Culture Brand.

If a team I'm working with hasn't nailed down their values yet, we start the discovery process by looking at what is frustrating people and what is celebrated to identify the organization's deeply held values. (Remember that clarifying your PV²M is a prerequisite to designing your Culture Brand.)

Don't rush through Bad Team or Bad Leader conversions here. Sit with them and think about qualities that can overcome the negative traits you've identified. As you look at the negatives as a whole, you will see all things that you wish would disappear forever from your organization. This step gets you closer to that reality.

Pro Tip: The practice of seeking out negatives helps identify some of the more important values. These Culture Brand characteristics become our actionable values. How will we act based on what we believe is important? Referring back to our discussion on deeply held values, those are often easier to find when we ask: What irritates you? The reason we are irritated and frustrated is that the behavior bumps up against our core values. Once you find the irritation, you can use that to find the positive value and behavior that overcomes it. These are often the most inspiring items in our lists.

Step Five: Choose Three Words

This is the moment you've been waiting for! In this step, you'll identify the three words that will capture your Culture Brand. Step back and look at the words in each category. Identify one word that communicates each area. You need one word for results, one for teaming, and one word for personal character.

Tips

- [ ] **Choose just one word for each category.** Yes, I know we are trying to say a lot with a single word. One step to help you get there is to identify the top three words first.

- [ ] **Look for "umbrella" words.** It's possible that you already have a few umbrella words up on the wall. These words capture or encompass the full meaning of the category, including those subcategory concepts. Recently, a team had *diligence* and *unselfish* in their lists, but they also saw the word *heart*. Heart was a word that could contain the ideas of diligence and selflessness at the same time. Heart was an umbrella word. As you consider the words to use, think about how you can shape a word or assign it a comprehensive definition.

- [ ] **Make it an action word.** Part of the challenge with values is that they are often ideas instead of actions. Find an action word like *drive* instead of *driven*, *aspire* instead of *aspiration*, or *innovate* instead of *innovation*.

- [ ] **Consider various definitions.** One team we work with chose the word *care* for character. A different organization chose *care* to represent teaming. In both cases, the teams made a strong case for the word choice and were able to implement *care* to express the meaning they wanted to convey.

- [ ] **Select a word that inspires you.** Your three Culture Brand words are most powerful when they are inspiring and captivating. They should ignite an emotional connection in you and your leadership team. Look for words that capture your heart.

- [ ] **Pack them with meaning.** Words have meanings, and words can be assigned meaning. You could choose three colors—blue, green, and orange—and then pack each of those words with meaning behind results, teaming, and character. The goal is to create a shortcut language that quickly means volumes of information for your organization.

☐ **Nine Subcategories for Reference.** One way to help your team understand the job of umbrella words is to show them the most common subcategories. Here they are again:

Results
- Goal-driven
- Pursues Excellence
- Holds Others Accountable

Teaming
- Collaborates
- Develops Others
- Encourages

Character
- Coachable
- Dependable
- Takes Ownership

☐ **Make it your own.** One of my clients chose *toughness* for their results category. The word resonated with the leadership team, particularly the business owner, who was a former college athlete, loved being outdoors, and whose family were rodeo enthusiasts.

One concern expressed during the discovery process was that toughness could potentially be misunderstood to mean that the leadership team expected everyone to just work harder. To make this word their own, the organization's onboarding for new team members now includes culture training. It's here that new team members learn that for this company, *toughness* means striving for excellence, using wisdom, and being willing to hold others accountable.

This team made *toughness* their own by packing it with deep meaning for this team. Today, they celebrate behaviors that demonstrate toughness as they work toward goals, quality, and holding one another accountable.

Code Blue vs. Blue Light Special
The Power of Shortcut Language

My wife is a nurse. I've been around medical terminology for over three decades now in our marriage. I've heard some crazy, amazing stories. One thing my vicarious medical training has taught me is the power of language.

In the medical field, speed can mean the difference between life and death. One of the most effective ways to increase speed is through quick and concise communication. In a hospital, the word "blue" is packed with meaning. When the "Code Blue" announcement comes through over the intercom, every staff member knows what is happening and what needs to happen immediately. Blue means that someone is in cardiac distress and that a pre-designated team needs to drop anything they are doing and move to the stated location. Action plans, crash carts, procedures, systems, and roles are in place so that the patient gets help right away. A life depends on that speed and efficiency, and it only takes the word *blue* to put everything in motion.

In another context, blue means something totally different. The last K-Mart store in the continental US closed in October 2024. Going to K-Mart was a weekly event for my family when I was a kid. My ten-year-old self could roam the departments of that store and dream so many dreams of toys, camping equipment, candy, or just stare in awe at the newest Sony Walkman displayed behind the glass cabinet.

K-Mart was known for its Blue Light Specials. About every thirty minutes, a flashing blue light would highlight a sales offer. You can't imagine the excitement and interest (and sales) this blue light created. It was a limited time, catch-it-now-or-never sale. Act fast! And people did.

In these two contexts, blue means two very different things. But if you know the culture in those organizations, you understand the meaning instantly. This is the kind of shortcut language we are working to develop for your organization.

Be Ready for Opposition

I've seen teams get stuck at different points while designing and implementing their Culture Brand, so I want to make you aware of a few potential obstacles and equip you to handle common objections.

"We've Got to Fix This, *Now*."

While creating the Bad Team and Bad Leader behavior lists, it's easy for people to get sidetracked by the negatives. Some on your leadership team may want to stop the meeting and immediately address or fix the problem. I've also had some leaders express frustration, saying I had too quickly flipped those negatives into positives during the exercise. They were struggling with the reality that those negative qualities existed in the organization, and they wanted solutions or a resolution right then.

If your meeting stalls here, I encourage you to address your team this way:

1. Admit that there are valid concerns and that the team is not yet where it needs to be.
2. Encourage your team to keep moving through the process by assuring them that the best way to stop bad behavior is to replace it with healthy behavior.
3. Commit to making the good behaviors nonnegotiable going forward.
4. Ask for their input on what they wish the organization could be. (Move to focusing on what you want instead of what you don't want.)

Democratizing Culture Upsets Some

Some people in the room will never fully buy into the idea of designing culture. Often, these holdouts see your new Culture Brand as a direct attack on the influence they have built within the organization. They may be unwilling to accept new ideas and will resist change because it means a loss of power for them.

With this exercise, you are democratizing culture, first by asking for input from your leadership team, and then by empowering all of your team members with clear, measurable standards for behavior. Everyone can begin evaluating where they are helping and where they are creating friction. You are putting the keys to culture into each person's hand and giving them the plan for winning and the authority to challenge others.

Defining Boundaries

If your culture has been undefined up to this point or developed by happenstance, it is likely that everyone in your organization has a slightly different understanding of what culture should be. This exercise with your leadership team gets everyone on the same page. As you draw clear boundary lines, people can see where they stand in relation to culture. They then have the option to either step into or out of the desired culture. Making the expectations clear eliminates needless conflict. At the same time, it can invite necessary conflict from those whose behavior doesn't align with your Culture Brand. That, too, is a good thing. It's okay to let people who are unwilling to step into the new culture exit (more on this in Chapter Six).

Dealing with the Doubters

By doing this exercise with your leadership team, you will (or should be) working with the best people in your organization. Almost everyone in the room really cares and will put their heart into the work. Sometimes, however, there are those on a team who aren't fully on board. Some may be skeptical and will opt to "wait and see" if this works before committing to implementing your Culture Brand. Others may have been burned by past experience with this group or another organization and may be unsure if anything can help.

If you find yourself facing these types of people, keep these principles in mind:

1. The goal is to accomplish the mission daily and achieve the vision together. Personal preferences do not override this.
2. Some people just need time and consistency to give their trust. Culture Brand can help you earn trust faster.

3. These people are worth the effort of winning over, but there comes a point where they may need to go. (More on this in Part Three of this book.)

Five Ways to Use Your Culture Brand

Here are some principles to keep in mind as you implement Culture Brand:

1. **It is a road map.** Having a Culture Brand is an instant gap analysis. It is the desired future reality that you begin using as a template for everyday behavior challenges. When something fits, you can say, "*This!* Keep this behavior!" "More like this!"

2. **It is a filter.** When something doesn't fit, you know it immediately, and you are able to determine the part of your culture that is missing in the particular behavior. For example, Bobby is dependably on time and gets his work done, but you noticed that his attitude changes from day to day. We need to be able to depend on Bobby's attitude. We can have a conversation about his dependability.

3. **It is a quick assessment.** When you are frustrated with a team member, you can run their behavior through the Culture Brand, and it will help you pinpoint the problem more quickly. You can then be more clear with your feedback.

4. **It is a starting line.** It gives you a place to start. Not everyone on your team fits your culture yet. But you can help them get there. Once you establish a clear picture of healthy team behavior, your team members will either select into the defined culture or opt out. Give your team members time to get there with regular accountability along the way. If they are unwilling to join, then they are opting out.

5. **It is a growth accelerator.** Culture Brand allows for growth and grace. Everyone on your team (including you) has cultural gaps in behavior. We are people. We all have room to grow. Emotional intelligence requires lifelong learning. Give your team a road map for winning at your culture.

Harness the Power of Culture

When you intentionally design your Culture Brand, you harness the power of a shared culture on a shared mission toward a shared vision. It's made even more powerful because you've created it together. You'll notice a sense of pride and confidence in your leaders emerge and lock the brand into place for everyone. Going forward, your leaders can speak with confidence that their directives represent the heart of what you are working to accomplish together.

With your Culture Brand, you . . .

- Make your values actionable and measurable.
- Map mission to moment-by-moment behavior.
- Raise the emotional and cultural intelligence of your organization.
- Create stronger clarity about behavior.
- Define what it takes to be a member of this culture.
- Make it easier for everyone to win and belong.
- Create a simple language for healthy leadership.
- Raise the potential for building trust throughout your organization.

Creating a Flat Culture

If you are the founder of your organization or you created your department from the ground up, you might remember a time early on when your business's culture didn't require design. It seemed instinctive and natural, as if everyone intuitively understood what was most important for the business. That initial core group had a strong sense of community. You experienced the tough early days together, and those shared experiences and values informed and governed everyone's behavior.

Once an organization grows beyond the leader's immediate influence, culture quickly deteriorates. With growth or attrition, the original library of knowledge, experience, and culture gets lost and diluted. These changes open the door for misunderstanding and disconnections that are hard to pinpoint. The only thing that is obvious is that your culture isn't what it used to be.

Culture Brand

Your Culture Brand gives you the ability to recapture what was lost. I call it creating a *flat culture*. With this clear and simple tool, you have shortened the cultural distance for everyone. Everyone is now accountable for these ideals, from the core leadership to the front of the organization—the most senior member to tomorrow's new hire. No one is exempt, and everyone has the authority to call out behavior that doesn't align with the culture.

Example

If *dependability* is an important characteristic, this behavior is expected in every role. Your first-level team member should be dependable at their level of responsibility in the organization, which might mean showing up on time and having a dependable attitude about work. As we move up the organizational chart to higher levels of leadership, this characteristic of being dependable expands to include the responsibilities of the role. Someone in management, for example, still needs to be dependable about their schedule and attitude, but now they also need to submit their budget proposals on time and be dependable about their commitments at the executive meetings. If we revisit the ladder example and remember that these are "left side of the ladder" topics that relate to culture and soft skills, it is interesting that all of the "left side" items are cumulative, while the hard skills on the "right side" are not. In other words, you can forget or lose competency from earlier roles on the right side (taking an order, speed on the production line), but you cannot forget "left side" behaviors, like being on time and having a dependable attitude as you move up the ladder.

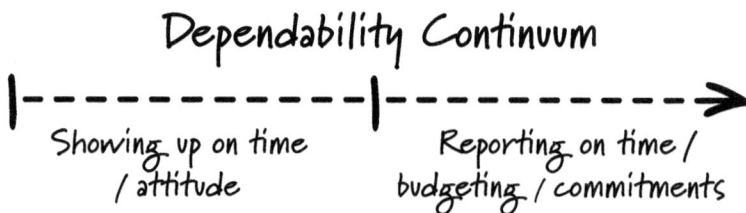

Dependability Continuum

|----------------|---------------->

Showing up on time / attitude

Reporting on time / budgeting / commitments

120

Culture Brand FAQs

Can I use words that others have already used?

Sure, but I've done this exercise scores of times now, and no one Culture Brand has been exactly the same. It's shocking, actually. I thought that at some point, things would get repetitive. The thing is, context matters. Each team is unique. Different backgrounds, experiences, personalities, and passions create different needs. There is something powerful about getting a group of leaders in a room and going through the sticky-note exercise. After wrestling with the concepts and agonizing over word choices, when teams find just the right words, it feels a bit magical. I guide and coax and challenge, but they hammer out the valuable words that fit their context. I will share an appendix of some of my favorite examples and some word lists to refer to, but I am purposely leaving it out of this space so that you can come to this exercise with a blank slate.

Is culture aspirational or attainable?

Leaders often ask if the words they choose for their Culture Brand can be aspirational or if they must be words that are (quickly) attainable. My answer is yes, both! They must also be nonnegotiable. Most often, the desired attributes are already within the organization, but they may not be ubiquitous or consistent.

Simplicity Is the Key

Culture Brand gives you a simple way to communicate your message and mission. There will be plenty of room in your Culture Brand to add detail and deeper development or application. Everything you want to add about leadership will nest within at least one of the three areas. One of the fascinating aspects of language is how meaning evolves and grows with usage. These terms become a shorthand language that communicates a wealth of knowledge, history, and intention. As your Culture Brand grows with you, it will provide a path to explore the comprehensive layers of culture within your organization.

But don't start by diving into the deep end of the pool. As you begin to broadcast your Culture Brand to the rest of your team, start simply. This is the key to organizational communication and unity. Begin by practicing your unique language—those three words that represent results, teaming, and character. Use them with your team every day. The more natural this language becomes, the stronger your culture will be.

Call to Action: Design Your Culture Brand

Set up a meeting with your leadership team and use the Culture Brand exercise outlined in this chapter.

Ask yourself and your team these questions:

1. How could our business look if we created a Culture Brand?

2. What could be different about my interaction with my leaders?

If you want support on this step, our team is ready to help you move forward with development and integration. Visit **leadersq.com/culture-brand** to learn more.

PART THREE:
LEADERS ALIGN CULTURE

You've got to connect before you correct.

Scott was surprised to see Ben, Intelex's VP of Sales, standing in line at The Coffee Nook on a busy Saturday morning. The man appeared uneasy—hands shoved into his pockets, gaze fixed on the pastry case.

When Ben reached the counter, he managed a tight smile.

"Do you have a few minutes?" he asked.

"Sure," Scott said. "Can I get you some coffee first? It's on the house."

A few minutes later, they sat at a corner table near the window, the morning sun glinting off polished wood. Ben stared at his cup for a long moment before speaking.

"I like your place," he said finally. "It's just like Kate described it. Everyone here seems . . . happy. They care about what they're doing."

"Thanks," Scott said. "I'm really glad you came in. Do you live out this way?"

"No." Ben shook his head. "I was driving. Thinking. And I realized I wasn't far from your shop. I figured I'd take the chance to see if you'd be around."

Scott waited, sensing that this visit wasn't about coffee.

Ben puffed out a deep breath, then said, "You know, I wasn't . . . receptive to your ideas the first time we met."

Scott smirked. "You aren't the only one."

Ben nodded, then looked down again. "I think I've really messed up."

Scott leaned back to give the young man room and said nothing.

Ben hesitated. "This stays between us?"

"Of course."

Ben rubbed the back of his neck. "I got together with another VP a while back—one who didn't like Kate's new direction. We were frustrated. He said this whole 'Advance, Elevate, Trust' thing was just another management fad."

He sighed. "I didn't agree—not completely anyway. But I didn't push back either. Then I went to my team of directors and tried to fix things on my own."

"How so?"

"Well, this sounds terrible, but I told them to ignore what Kate said. I figured she was going to leave or get fired, just like the rest of the CEOs who have come and gone before her." He sighed. "Historically, Intelex has been tough on its leaders. Expectations are high, so they either burn out, get replaced, or both, and all of them come in with their own agendas, trying to 'fix' things, but nothing ever changes. Until now."

Scott nodded thoughtfully, then asked, "So you're thinking now that Kate might be the exception to that rule?"

"I do. Now. But our sales team was struggling. We needed to hit our numbers, and I thought that it would be better to focus on keeping morale high rather than worry about tracking the metrics. I thought if I could keep everyone happy, the results would follow." He sighed. "Turns out I was wrong. Our numbers continued to decline. The other departments are frustrated with my team, and I don't blame them."

You've got to connect before you correct.

Ben paused and turned the cup without picking it up.

"There's more," he added quietly. "That other VP, he mentioned you. Said he knew a guy you used to work with. Told me you'd washed out and opened a coffee shop because you couldn't cut it in corporate."

Scott didn't flinch. "I've heard worse."

Ben looked up. "Is it true?"

Scott shrugged. "Depends on how you define washed out. I failed plenty. But I learned to lead better because of it. If failure's part of the tuition, then I suppose I paid my fees."

Ben gave a weak laugh. "I didn't see how Kate was going to pull all this together. Now I wish I hadn't said anything to my team. She's really doing it, and I feel like I've betrayed her trust."

"Does Kate know?"

He shook his head.

"What do you think will happen if you don't tell her?"

Ben stared at the table. "I'm not sure I could stay. It would feel like living a lie."

"And if you do tell her?"

He sighed. "She might fire me. And if she doesn't, I don't know how she could ever trust me again."

Scott folded his hands. "I can't guarantee how she'll react. But if I were her, and you came clean, I'd count that as a win. She probably already senses the distrust, but maybe not the source. You could help relieve that weight—and reset your influence with your team at the same time."

Ben frowned. "You mean tell them too?"

"I would," Scott said. "Apologize. Own your mistake. Let them see what alignment looks like."

Ben sat back, considering. "That's probably the best way to make it right."

Scott smiled. "I've found confession's a decent fertilizer. It's messy, but it helps things grow."

Ben chuckled softly. The weight he was carrying seemed to lighten a little.

"Can I get you a refill?" Scott asked.

"Yes, please."

Ben watched the easy rhythm between Scott and his team—the quick glances, the quiet efficiency, the way they smiled when he passed by.

When Scott returned, Ben said, "You know, you don't seem very commanding. How do you get them to work so hard when you're always so . . . nice?"

Scott grinned. "Ha! Fair question. It's something I've struggled with. For a long time, kindness got me into trouble. I let people slide because I didn't want to seem harsh. I ended up doing half their work myself. It was a broken way to lead. I confused being liked with being effective."

He leaned forward. "Remember my story about the library?"

Ben nodded.

"Well, when I sorted all those books into piles, I realized I'd avoided the whole stack on results. I liked reading about relationships and character, but not outcomes. Eventually, I was strong on teaming and character—but weak on results. That imbalance nearly cost me the business."

Scott stood and walked over to the counter. When he came back, he carried two small cups—one empty, one filled with coffee beans.

"These," he said, setting them down, "represent two types of leadership."

He pointed to the full cup. "This cup represents positional leadership— authority. When you give a directive, you're taking beans out of this cup.

You've got to connect before you correct.

The problem is, you can only make withdrawals. If all you do is command and control, you'll empty the cup. Eventually, the team stops listening. They may fire their boss and leave—or worse, fire their boss and stay."

He tapped the empty cup. "This one represents relational leadership. It starts out empty. Before you withdraw anything, you have to make deposits—investing in people, knowing them, coaching them, and celebrating their wins. Every time you encourage, correct well, or show care, you add beans. Then, when you need something big—an extra shift, a hard deadline—they'll follow you because they trust you."

Ben studied the cups. "I like that. But I'd worry people might take advantage of that trust. They might act compliant just to stay in my good graces. Then it looks like I'm showing favoritism."

Scott nodded. "That's possible. But here's the balance—you still have authority beans. If someone misuses your kindness, you pull from the first cup. You say, 'I'd rather lead through trust, but you've forced me to lead through authority.' It's a reset. And when the behavior changes, you can go back to making deposits again."

"I've been living in the relational cup." Ben sighed then said, "I thought if I just kept everyone happy, we'd be fine. But I let accountability slide."

Scott smiled. "You're not alone. I did the same thing for years. The trick is to lead from both cups. You've got to connect before you correct. That's how you align people around culture. You hold them accountable not just to you and your expectations but more importantly to the culture *because* you care about the team, the individual, and the results you're achieving together."

Ben looked at him for a long time, then nodded slowly. "I needed to hear that."

"Then go make it right," Scott said. "With Kate—and with your team. Tell them the truth. Call them up, not out. You'll be surprised how ready people are to follow a leader who owns his mistakes."

Culture Brand

Ben exhaled, something like peace crossing his face. "Thank you. Really. I'll do it."

"Good," Scott said, grinning. "And next time, the coffee's on you."

Ben laughed. "Deal."

Chapter 6
Call People Up

*Culture is what happens when the
CEO isn't in the room.*
—Peter Drucker

As a culture leader, your role is to help your team members join you on the mission. Remember: Culture drives mission; in fact, it can powerfully support and enhance every aspect of your PV²M. But your team can only harness that momentum when everyone is aligned in purpose, values, vision, mission, *and* culture.

Now that you've designed your Culture Brand, you can use it to bring everyone into alignment. The previous chapters laid a great deal of groundwork to get to this moment, where the Culture Brand tool becomes incredibly practical. So, let's get right to the heart of this chapter. Then we'll explore alignment a little more deeply and what it means to call people up. In previous chapters, I've listed all sorts of benefits of Culture Brand:

- It sets the expectation for how you will work together.
- It defines success and outlines how you want to represent the organization to your clients, vendors, and community.
- It is a three-word culture "guidebook" that helps you and your team members stay focused on the mission.
- It also ensures that no one personality is responsible for driving or capable of derailing that mission.

So let's talk about *how* this tool can do all of those things.

Coaching with Culture Brand

Culture Brand is not about having three more words to paint on the wall. It's a tool that is meant to be actionable. One of the best ways to use it is during your one-on-one meetings with your team members—starting with the leadership team. Lead out loud by using the Culture Brand Assessment tool with them. You can use the QR code to download the coaching tool, or take out a sheet of paper and draw your own, adding in your organization's Culture Brand words.

Download a PDF of the 1:1 Coaching Tool Here

Self-Assessment
(Rate each behavior 1–10)

- Goal-driven
- Pursues Excellence
- Holds Others Accountable

- Collaborates
- Encourages
- Develops Others

(Results) (Teaming)

(Character)

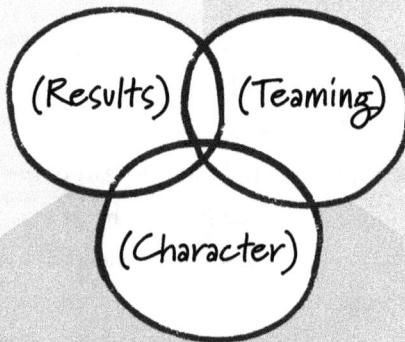

- Coachable
- Dependable
- Takes Ownership

Complete the assessment for yourself and ask each team member to do the same.

1. Each person should evaluate themselves first, assigning a score between one and ten in each of the nine areas. Ten is outstanding; a one denotes a complete lack or disregard for the behavior.

2. Come to the coaching session prepared to share your self-evaluation with the other person.

3. Discuss what they've identified about themselves.

   Your conversation might sound something like this:

   Person A: Shares a high-scored area.

   Person B: "Yes, I have observed you doing that, and it is so helpful. Just the other day, [insert a specific and recent example of that behavior]."

   Person A: Shares a low-scored area.

   Person B: "Thank you for sharing that. What is one way I can help you grow in that area in the next two weeks?"

The actual conversation may sound something like this:

Leader: What is an area you feel really good about?

Team Member: Well, one of my highest scores is goal-driven.

Leader: That is really important for our organization. I've seen you do that well. You've hit your target almost every day this month. (Give specific examples when you can.)

Leader: We're always striving to grow. What is an area you feel you need to improve in?

Team Member: Collaboration is an area where I'm not as strong. It just feels easier to do things myself. I'm not great at asking for help.

Leader: Thank you for sharing that. I would love to help you with that area. You are really great at setting and achieving goals. What's a goal you would like to set for practicing collaboration in the next two weeks?

Any leadership role feels heavier when you have to be the behavior police. Calling people out on their toxic behavior gets old really fast as a supervisor. (It is more challenging when you're addressing a peer or you're a subordinate speaking to someone in a higher position on the organizational chart.) Here is what I propose: Call people up instead of calling them out.

Designing a Culture Brand is a way to establish a culture code for a healthy environment in which your business and every person in it can thrive. No matter what your leadership status is, when you point out someone's

> ## Call people up instead of calling them out.

negative or destructive attitudes and behaviors, the criticism immediately puts that person on the defensive. Calling your team member or coworker to rise to a higher standard is a more positive and hopeful approach. It is a way of saying, *I believe in you. I can help you get there.* It also opens the door for honest conversations where people can admit, *I struggle with this too. Can we work on this together?*

Calling people up rather than calling them out is one of my favorite benefits of having a Culture Brand. I really don't like holding people accountable (Yes! That's one of my low-score areas), but I find that this approach couches accountability with strong support. It says, "We are human, and we are on a journey. Can I help you lift this load until you can carry it on your own?" It also gives people the tools to hold *themselves* accountable.

Engage People in Culture-Focused Conversations

When we call people up, we can begin our coaching by focusing on strengths. Please understand, I am not talking about delivering the stale *feedback sandwich*—the technique many leaders were taught to rely on for giving tough feedback. You know the one: say something nice, then give the correction, then say something else nice. The problem with the feedback sandwich is that it ends up feeling inauthentic. People see right through the tactic and completely ignore the two compliments.

The Culture Brand coaching method increases self-awareness, which highlights the authenticity of your feedback, giving more weight and value to your encouraging words.

Pouring In vs. Drawing Out

Leaders are charged with developing their team members, and much of the language around this idea sounds like *pouring into, investing in,* or *inspiring* people. Certainly, there is value in pouring into people, but at some point, leaders need to be able to shift toward *drawing out* the best in others. This shift is important because it takes some of the burden off leaders' shoulders and honors the other person's strengths and abilities.

I've had several leaders tell me that they are "just not good at being inspirational." My challenge to those leaders—and to you if you feel the same way—is to consider whether inspiration is what's necessary for your team's success. Inspiration implies that the leader is the source of energy and growth. To create cultural momentum, you need people to bring *their* best and be their own source of motivation.

Instead of trying to pour into or inspire people, consider how you can change your language and shift your focus to discovering gifts and shaping or unleashing people's potential. Ask: *What are the incredible resources in the people around me? How can I pull those resources together into the mission that we share?*

Awareness Through Self-Reflection

Self-assessment is the primary way to use the Culture Brand with team members. I recommend that both you and the person you are developing complete the Culture Brand Assessment. When reviewing the criteria, the question to ask is, *How does my behavior fit with our Culture Brand?*

With your completed evaluations in hand, discuss the observations. *Pro Tip:* You go first. It sets the tone for how the exercise works and introduces your vulnerability in an area for growth. You are creating a learning environment by being transparent and coachable.

When you share with your team member how you scored *yourself* in the nine areas, let them see where you think you are strong and where you feel you need to grow. This transparency helps to open the door for a conversation about development. No leader has it all together. If your team member has been around you for any time, any weakness you reveal will probably not be much of a surprise. If what you reveal as an area of growth does surprise your team member, the act of vulnerability only further demonstrates your authenticity, which builds trust in the relationship. That trust emboldens others to be authentic and vulnerably honest with you.

When I introduce this coaching exercise in leadership team workshops, I ask the participants to get into pairs and practice complimenting and calling up the other person.

Currency of Trust

Trust is hard to build and easy to lose. Studies have shown that low-trust environments have a high overall cost to the business. Conversely, high-trust organizations have been able to reduce business costs. Trust helps us all move faster and more efficiently. Use the Culture Brand to build trust between team members and between levels of the organization.

Step 1: Compliment a strength. Look at the top-rated categories and say, "I do see this in you. Just the other day, I saw you _____ (fill in the blank with a specific example of this behavior). That quality is so important for our organization/team."

Step 2: Call the person up. Look for the lowest numbers and ask, "Which of these would you like to work on over the next two weeks? I would love to support your growth in one of them and help you track progress."

After the participants shared their assessments with their partners, I asked, "What were the feelings and emotions that you had while you shared your assessment?" Their responses speak to the benefits of this approach:

"I felt vulnerable."

"I felt encouraged."

"It was easy to talk about my weaknesses."

"I was surprised at how much alike we are."

"I was surprised to learn how different we are."

"I had rated myself low, and they encouraged me to raise my score."

As we talk through these reactions, the leaders in the room inevitably observe the low defenses in the conversations. Calling out coworkers causes stress and often leads to shutting down or defensiveness. Self-assessments open the door for real conversations, as well as helpful, supportive interaction. When people feel stressed or threatened, the body and brain react in ways that are counterproductive to growth and development. This coaching process helps keep stress lower, which allows people to be more emotionally connected for growth and support. It is not a feedback sandwich. It is a rich and genuine conversation.

Responding to Incorrect Self-Assessments

When individuals score their behaviors on a scale of one to ten, it is a very real possibility that they will assess themselves incorrectly in some areas. It's to be expected, in fact, and doesn't negate the power of the Culture Brand coaching method. Keep in mind that the scoring is subjective and relative. With the scale ranging from one to ten, some people will score themselves high, and others will give themselves a lower score than they might give their peer who has similar strength. Each person's personality and perspective drives those subjective answers—so, too, does their experience level, role, and level of responsibility within the organization.

For leaders, the win is not in the accuracy of someone's self-assessment scores but in the relativity of them.

We can almost always affirm and celebrate something from an area that a person self-assesses as a strength. And any one score that is even slightly lower gives us an opening to talk about it as a developmental opportunity.

Here are a few additional suggestions for responding to self-assessments that don't measure up to what you're seeing in the team member:

- **Go with what they give, at least at first.** In your first one-on-one, consider just going with the scores they give themselves. Earn the right to say the harder things in a future conversation by working with them where they think they are.

- **Ask for examples.** When people give themselves a score that you think is way off, ask them to share an example of that behavior from the last few weeks. It's possible that they may surprise you with a scenario you were unaware of. It's also possible their scenario will not fit the definition. In this case, you can help them understand what the term means. Or they may realize that they can't give you an example and end up changing the rating.

- **Define your answers.** When the scores are way off, often it's because there is a misunderstanding. They see *collaborate* on the sheet and assume they are collaborating, when actually they are telling others what to do and not really listening to others. It may be that their idea of collaborating is not in agreement with what we need. Take this time to redefine, with examples, what productive collaboration is.

- **Meet in the middle.** Sometimes the disparity in scoring is related to personality. A perfectionist may resist higher scores, while an optimist may overscore. The truth is sometimes in the middle. Negotiating these scores can be a productive exercise in clarifying expectations; for example, if they rate themselves as highly dependable, but you can't remember the last time they showed up on time or turned in their work on time, don't just shut them down by saying, "You're so wrong!" Simply say: "I see you put a score of eight on dependability. What are some examples of eight out of ten behavior for this dependability? How would your coworkers rate you in this area, and how would they prove their score?"

A Growth Environment

We are not aiming for perfection; we are aiming for awareness and growth. Progress is success; stagnation is failure. Creating a psychologically safe environment for self-assessment opens the door for awareness and a desire

> We are not aiming for perfection; we are aiming for awareness and growth. Progress is success; stagnation is failure.

to grow. It's like putting seeds in good soil. Healthy environments foster growth. This next section explores a few more ways to use your Culture Brand to create a healthy team environment.

Culture Fit vs. Culture Add

There has been a great deal of discussion around the problems with organizations pursuing *culture fit* in hiring. The concern is that in seeking to find people who *fit*, the pendulum swings against diversity, which can be harmful to individuals as well as to the organization. Diversity—of backgrounds, education, life experiences, and thought—gives teams a powerful advantage. Having a variety of perspectives and personalities invites healthy conflict by bringing different ideas and voices to the table.

Rather than looking for culture *fit*, I think we need to be looking for culture *add* by asking questions like these:

- How do the people on our team add to or enhance the culture?
- What voices or perspectives are missing from our team?
- How will this potential new hire's voice bring a different perspective and help us live into our PV²M?

When organizations use Culture Brand with a focus on culture *add*, they seek out and promote people not because they *fit* but because they bring out the best in everyone. The goal is *not* to create an echo chamber of the leader's voice, but to build a strong, healthy team composed of diverse perspectives, personalities, and strengths. In light of this conversation about culture fit, let's look for ways we can bring people into the team who add to our culture without detracting from the mission.

How to Belong Here

Having a clear and attainable culture allows the possibility for anyone to belong. Rather than overriding individualism and creating clones, it celebrates each person's unique contribution and identifies opportunities for growth. This is how we create synergistic organizations, where one plus one equals more than two. We are better together because we complement each other and make up for where others lack.

Calling people up is about creating awareness around strengths and weaknesses and then challenging people to grow in both. Culture Brand encourages each person to own their behavior in a way that is healthy for the organization.

As a culture leader, you set the standard and the example with your Culture Brand as the guide. Neglecting any one of the three essential areas of results, teaming, or character works against the mission. Nobody is perfect, but because all three areas are nonnegotiable, no one gets a pass by saying,

"That's just how I am." Telling people to accept us as we are is not a growth mindset. A growth mindset says: *Accept me for who I can become.*

Fostering Accountability

Accountability isn't a single action—it's two distinct behaviors. I like to think of it as the *Rope of Accountability.* Some leaders take this rope and tie others up, dragging them from task to task. The problem? The leader is doing all the work, while the follower feels micromanaged and disengaged.

A healthier way to create an environment of accountability is for the leader to offer one end of that rope to the team member. When the other person accepts it, they are saying that they are willing to take responsibility or ownership of their behavior.

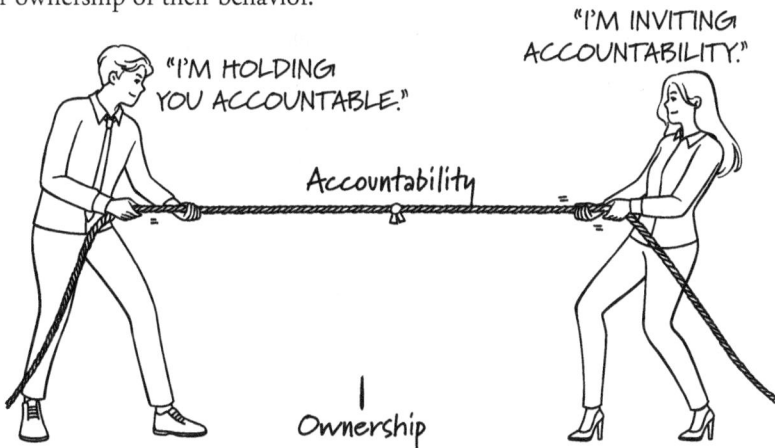

"I'M HOLDING YOU ACCOUNTABLE."

"I'M INVITING ACCOUNTABILITY."

Accountability

Ownership

The leader can keep the rope short at first—checking in, offering support, and holding them accountable with gentle tugs. But accountability isn't just about the leader pulling someone along. The follower can also tug on that rope by saying, "I need help," or "I'm finished." Or they might say, "I don't understand," or "I am 30 percent done. Please take a look at my progress."

Learn more about the Rope of Accountability Tool

The real shift happens when those tugs increase from the follower's side. That's the moment ownership transfers. If accountability only moves in one direction, it remains control. When it moves both ways, it becomes true ownership and collaboration.

A growth environment requires this shift to personal ownership. This goes back to that idea of pouring into people or drawing out their best. Yes, as leaders, we must invest in people, but accountability is always a two-sided relationship.

Growing and Letting Go

All good leaders care about the people on their teams. We want to help others grow; in fact, we see it as our responsibility to bring out their best. We operate from the mindset that everyone can change and grow.

Are people worth our time and energy? Absolutely! People are the most valuable resource in the universe. When you make the effort to identify and address negative behavior quickly (while it is correctable), you can also measure how receptive the person is to change. Give them time, training, and coaching, and realize that at some point, you may need to decide that you've

> The unfortunate reality is that while everyone can change and grow, not everyone will be able to do it within your timeline.

given them enough time and recognize that they are choosing not to align the organization's culture. The unfortunate reality is that while everyone can change and grow, not everyone will be able to do it within your timeline. You can't *control* the people you are developing. Neither can you control all the factors in their lives. Sometimes, no matter how hard you try, there will be people who either refuse to take responsibility for their growth or are unable to make the changes required. When that's the case, delaying the inevitable, allowing negative or toxic behavior to persist, or making allowances just to keep that person with the company only makes a bad situation worse.

A business owner reached out to me recently because he was struggling with a team member. The leadership team had invested considerable time and effort trying to develop this person's teaming behaviors. After many months, there had been some small progress, but not enough to justify more or greater effort. Despite repeated coaching, the consequence of this person's anti-culture behavior was toxic. The business owner wanted to keep the individual on the team because of the person's unique skills and the significant results they brought to the organization. The owner even considered creating a special role for this person as a way to keep them in the organization—but not on any team. Notice, it wasn't the hard skill but the culture gaps that caused the issues.

"What is best for the business?" I asked the business owner. "Is this solution for the business or for this person?"

The question of *what's best for the business* is one that must be asked. When growth is not proportional to the time and energy invested, we must evaluate the cost. How is that person's refusal to grow affecting the rest of the team, the clients, or the organization? Are we carving out protected cultural space for a person to allow behavior to continue in a controlled environment, or is there a point where we need to let that person go because the effort to protect the culture from them is over-indexed?

Exiting team members is never easy, but it becomes more challenging when we wait too long. In walking with clients through these tough situations, I have observed a few reasons that leaders delay in exiting toxic team members.

The toxic team member gets results. They are either individually productive or their destructive methods (usually fear tactics) motivate others to produce. Fear erodes trust. The person may achieve quick, short-term payoffs of productivity. These results can seduce leaders into ignoring the abusive behavior or even covering it up.

The toxic team member is deeply integrated into the business. If the person has been with the company for a long time or has extensive, even exclusive, operational knowledge, losing their information and experience could leave a noticeable void. Countless clients of ours have reflected on this delayed approach and wish they had acted sooner. The team typically responds positively when toxic people are removed. It is as if they have been holding their breath for too long, and there is a renewed sense of relief in their demeanor. It may also mean that others will follow the toxic person out of the organization, but this is also a healthy removal of an unhealthy subculture.

The leader takes undue responsibility for the toxic team member's bad behavior. Good leaders want to see people succeed. I've seen leaders delay, holding on to the hope that if they (the leader) just try harder or give the team member more time and more chances to change, the destructive behavior will stop.

None of these reasons, however, is worth risking the culture and growth environment you're working to create.

It takes time, consistency, and alignment to firmly establish a Culture Brand, and it's the leader's responsibility to protect it once it is built. Engaging people in culture-focused conversations and making everyone aware of what behaviors align and *don't* align with your desired culture fosters an environment where people can grow.

With the self-assessment tools and regular coaching, you'll know by the person's behavior if they have been receptive to feedback and made changes—or not. You will also have a record of how hard you (or someone on your leadership team) worked to help the individual overcome their negative behavior. And when someone refuses to support the culture and the mission, the clear standards you've set forth with your Culture Brand equip you with the necessary data to move more quickly and with greater confidence to exit people who are toxic to the organization.

Call to Action: Create Better Reviews

Use the self-evaluation guide that was provided for the 1:1 coaching session. Think of someone you have exited from the organization for any reason. Use the guide to evaluate the person's cultural fit and misfit. Think through the following questions as a way to consider how you might use this guide in a future situation.

- Where was this individual strong? How did those strengths make it harder for you to let them go?

- Where were they inconsistent? Often in exits, you have individuals who fluctuate in their strong/weak behaviors. What influenced those fluctuations?

- Where was this person weak?

Now, consider how you could incorporate the Culture Brand targets into your performance review system. Examine the current way you are measuring performance and see if there are ways to improve your review system with these behavior areas. You may find that your current review questions are out of balance in one or more areas of the Culture Brand. It is natural for organizations to drift toward results or relationships.

Change the people, or change the people.

The culture at Intelex had improved. Kate could feel it—fewer fires to put out, more honest conversations, real ownership. Ben was proof of that. He'd stood in front of his team, owned the way he'd undermined Kate's direction, apologized, and reset expectations around their culture—to Advance, Elevate, and Trust. Within a month, his numbers had recovered, and he had worked to regain her trust.

Todd was another story.

The first warning sign was a missed deadline. Then another. When a product rollout stalled because two departments hadn't coordinated, Kate traced the breakdown to operations—Todd's division.

She'd asked him to come to her office on Friday afternoon in hopes of getting to the root of the problem before the weekend. She looked up when he knocked on the door frame.

"Hi, Todd," she said. "Come on in."

When he didn't close the door behind him, she got up and closed it herself, then motioned to a chair.

He didn't sit.

"Marketing says they never got the updated specs," she said as she returned to her desk.

"Then marketing's lying. My team delivered."

The defensiveness hit like déjà vu—old patterns she thought they'd outgrown. "This isn't about who's right," she said. "It's about how we work together. We don't win by accident. We win by alignment."

He checked his phone and abruptly turned to leave. "I've got a meeting."

The door clicked shut before she could reply.

That night at home, Kate stared at the ceiling and considered all the ways she might be failing him. Had she been unclear or unsupportive? She didn't think so. Too quick to expect change? It had been almost nine months already, and the rest of the leadership team was on board.

What am I missing? What am I doing wrong?

By morning, she knew she needed perspective.

The Coffee Nook was calm after the rush. She walked in to the sounds of steam hissing and ceramic dishes clinking. After ordering her drink, Kate sat at a table near the window. A few moments later, Scott slid a cortado in front of her and sat.

"Rough few days?" he asked.

"Rough few weeks," she said. "Thanks for making time to talk."

"Happy to," Scott replied. "What's going on?"

"Well, truthfully, it isn't all bad. Ben owned his part, and he's turned things around in his department."

Scott smiled. "That's good to hear. He seems to be all-in on seeing Intelex succeed."

Kate nodded, then blew out a sigh. "Todd, on the other hand, is another story. He's brilliant—no one questions that—but he's . . .

corrosive. I keep thinking I can reach him if I just keep investing. But every time I try, he doubles down on his way of doing things."

As he had with Ben, Scott shared the illustration of the two cups—the authority cup (positional power) and the relationship cup (earned trust).

"I've been living out of the relationship cup with Todd," she said. "I keep making deposits, but nothing sticks."

Scott tilted his head. "Then it's time to use the other cup. Clear standards. Clear consequences. You lead with trust, but you protect culture with authority."

They sat quietly for a moment, sipping their coffee. Scott chuckled softly.

"What is it?" Kate asked.

"Another plant lesson I learned from Clark a few months back. This time it was right here."

"At the shop?"

"Yeah. Clark came to town to see the grandkids—and drink his way through the menu," Scott began.

Kate saluted that thought by raising her cup, then taking another sip.

"One morning, I found him kneeling in the flower bed just over there." He pointed to a large flowerbed on the other side of the glass. "He was elbow deep in the soil, digging around a small ornamental tree. When I asked what he was doing, he said, 'This one's not growing like the others.'

"I told him I didn't know why not. They all went in the ground at the same time, just before we opened the shop, and the other trees were doing just fine."

"I bet Clark knew why," Kate chimed in.

"Well, not at first, but he went and found a shovel and did some digging. A few hours later, he opens the door, overalls covered in dirt, and waves at me to come outside. There was a big hole where the tree had been, and at the bottom was a slab of concrete. A cistern cap."

Kate's eyes widened.

Scott affected his voice to sound like Clarks, "'Old property, old surprises. You could water that tree for ten years, and it wouldn't put down roots here.'"

"So what did he do?" Kate asked.

"Moved it," Scott said. "His advice was to find a new spot for it. If it's a healthy tree, it should take root in the new location. He also said if the tree didn't grow well there, it wasn't worth the work to keep trying to save it."

Kate nodded with understanding. "So, following the analogy through, sometimes people need a new role or a different team or leader to help them grow. But sometimes, it doesn't matter what you do; the person isn't going to thrive."

"Yep. And if the latter is the case with Todd, the kindest thing you can do for him and the rest of the team is to stop pretending that water will fix the concrete."

Kate sat with that for a long moment. "I want to believe I can develop anyone."

"You can develop anyone who is willing," Scott said gently. "Culture works when someone engages it. With Todd, the question isn't 'Can he?' It's 'Will he?'"

She nodded, jaw set. "Then I owe him clarity."

Kate started with coaching—real coaching, not wishful thinking. She met with Todd one-on-one and laid out a crisp plan:

Advance (Results): deliver weekly cross-functional plans before work begins; no launches without shared timelines and signed specs.

Change the people, or change the people.

Elevate (Teaming): delegate decisions, not tasks; bring two peers into your weekly stand-ups to increase transparency.

Trust (Character): no blame language; if you're late, you own it publicly and reset expectations.

"I'll support you," she said. "I'll meet with you every Friday for six weeks. At the end, we'll review outcomes against these standards."

Todd's nod was slow, unreadable. "Fine," he said. "If it gets you off my back."

Week one: silence from operations until two days before a launch.

Week two: a late-night email chain blaming marketing.

Week three: a stand-up where Todd's managers spoke only when spoken to.

Kate tried a different approach: move the tree. She offered a role shift—fewer people, more technical scope, a peer leader with strong EQ to model the behaviors Todd resisted.

He folded his arms. "You're demoting me?"

"Finding a better fit for you," she countered. "You're exceptional at systems. We need to leverage that strength."

He stood. "I'm not the problem here."

Kate stood her ground. After making it clear that the new role was his only option for staying with Intelex, he agreed. Begrudgingly.

Within two weeks of moving Todd into his new role, two resignation letters from promising managers had landed in Kate's inbox. Both cited the same reason: "hostility in the workplace."

Kate stared at the screen until the words steadied. Water wasn't going to fix concrete.

HR scheduled the meeting for late that afternoon. Todd arrived smiling, casual.

"What's up, boss?"

Culture Brand

Kate folded her hands on the desk. Calm. Clear. "Todd, you're extraordinary at operations. But how you drive results is hurting the organization. We gave coaching. We offered a role that leveraged your strengths with less harm to people. You declined. We're at a crossroads."

He scoffed. "So, what? Results don't matter anymore?"

"They do," she said. "So do people. Our culture is Advance, Elevate, Trust. We can't sacrifice any one of the three without sacrificing the whole. I'm ending your employment today."

He stared at her, incredulous. "You're going soft."

Kate stood, signaling the meeting was over. "No. We're growing strong."

That evening, Kate called Scott. "I let Todd go," she said.

A pause. "Letting someone go never gets easy," he said. "But I'm proud of you."

"It doesn't feel good."

"It's not supposed to," he said. "It's supposed to feel right."

As word of Todd's exit spread over the next few days, the mood in the building shifted.

Culture wasn't a memo anymore. It was a mirror.

Over the next month, leaders repeated the three words— Advance, Elevate, Trust—and asked their teams how their decisions reflected the culture. For her part, Kate offered clarity for everyone by formalizing what her team had been practicing:

Replicate language—Every leader opened staff meetings with a sixty-second culture story—one win in each domain.

Replicate behaviors—Peer-shadowing across departments would help transfer teaming habits, not just process.

Replicate leaders—Promotions would require evidence on both sides of the ladder of development: hard skills and people skills.

And when someone wasn't thriving, leaders asked the three questions first: Wrong soil? Wrong seat? Concrete? Move when possible; exit when necessary.

Change the people, or change the people.

"Change the people, or change the people," a phrase she had resisted, became something of a motto.

She didn't mean discard people. She meant call them up—and when they refuse to rise to expectations of the culture, protect the garden.

Their culture had finally, truly transformed, and the timing proved providential. She'd received a call from the board. A merger was on the horizon. And alignment—the kind that could replicate leader to leader and team to team—would be the only way through.

Chapter 7
Creating a Culture-Driven People Strategy

Shaping your culture is more than half done when you hire your team.

—Jessica Herrin

Have you ever had the sensation of being in a new place or with a new group where you immediately felt a sense of belonging—a place where the people, their attitude, and the atmosphere provided a sense of normalcy, even comfort, despite the newness? Those are the places where you feel as if you've been there forever—in a *good* way.

Compare that to the feeling of visiting a country whose customs and culture are very different from yours. The language is different, the food is different, people dress differently, and *everything* feels unfamiliar. Even if you are happy to be there, you are persistently aware that you are an outsider.

One of the hardest parts of joining a new group is learning the unwritten social rules. Part of the work of establishing your Culture Brand is to make those "rules" visible, thereby lowering the barriers to belonging. One way you can do that is by creating a flat culture. I introduced this concept of flat culture back in Chapter Five. I want to come back to it here because it is an essential first step in developing a culture-driven people strategy.

In unhealthy organizations, the rules for culture vary depending on a person's position in the company hierarchy. In these organizations, subcultures develop and create division and distrust.

Now, please note that I am not implying that we should do away with organizational charts. Most uses of the term *flat culture* are about removing hierarchies or management layers to increase decision-making efficiency. Structure is necessary for role clarity and the distribution of responsibility. What I *am* saying is that even the largest organizational chart can and should be culturally flat, in that any team member should be able to expect like behavior from every other team member. A flat culture calls for everyone to behave appropriately within the culture creed because those rules serve as the authority over every position equally. The outcome is a sense of loyalty, mutual respect, and trust. You can see this effect in military circles and among college alumni, where shared ideals create a bond.

The point of a flat culture is to create consistent standards, from the top of the career ladder to the first rung, but that isn't to say that those at the higher levels don't have greater responsibility. They do; in fact, in a culture-driven organization, the behavior at the top of the ladder matters even more.

Greater Responsibility, Greater Impact

The culture may be flat, but the organization is not. While every member of the organization is expected to live up to the same cultural standards, the behavior at the top of the ladder will always have greater impact—for good or for ill. All eyes are on the top leaders as models of culture. This reality means that those at the top must uphold the Culture Brand with diligence. When leaders fail to honor the culture, their behavior signals that it is not as important as everyone says or that some people are exempt from good culture behavior.

Let's use this example. Suppose you are on a hike with friends, and you are walking along a path through the forest. If you stumbled on a small stone, probably only the person right behind you would notice. Others in the group may never know that your toe caught and kicked a small rock across the path. But if you are leading this same group on a hike along a steep, high-mountain trail, one relatively small stone disturbed when you stumble could roll down the narrow path, knock loose a few other stones as it gathers momentum, and cause a chain reaction of falling rocks that could be disastrous for those behind you on the trail.

These small stones represent your behaviors and words. They seem insignificant to you, but they take on greater gravity as they travel through the team. Anti-cultural behavior can take on momentum and result in a damaging message about your attitude toward the culture. If those same behaviors are mimicked by your team members, the harm can be almost irrevocable. Be open and vulnerable about your missteps.

Are you and those on your leadership team going to make cultural missteps from time to time? Almost certainly. Humility and transparency can limit the damage and help you restore trust. Being vulnerable enough to share your self-assessment with your team members is one simple and powerful way to acknowledge any failings and demonstrate your commitment to the Culture Brand.

Cascade Your Culture

The good news is that just as a leader's negative behaviors and words can cause significant damage when they are repeated by those further down the organizational chart, positive behaviors and words can help ensure that the desired culture cascades through the organization. While we are aiming to create a flat culture where everyone is accountable (up and down on the organizational chart) to live and work by the same culture and values, organizations are hierarchical in nature. Organizational culture, however, should transcend hierarchy. Otherwise, it will erode trust in the organization.

One of the beautiful things about creating a Culture Brand is that it makes it possible for everyone to understand what the culture should be. It's a way to clearly express the heart of the business to new team members and leaders. Likewise, it boosts leaders' confidence as they encourage and enforce the desired behaviors.

The consistent messaging of your Culture Brand reduces the confusion that exists when competing voices are speaking into a team member's performance. If a team member has a leader who values high results above all else and a coworker who expects high relationships, it will feel impossible to live up to both expectations. Feeling pulled in different directions is frustrating. Your Culture Brand equips team members and leaders with a clear standard and reminds those competing voices that healthy cultures consist of relationships *and* results.

Once your Culture Brand is established, it doesn't take long for people to catch on. In one organization we worked with, the business owner took time to explain the culture to a group of new team members during the onboarding process. After they'd been working with the company for a few weeks, one of the mid-level managers was behaving rather harshly toward the new hires. One of those new team members turned to that middle manager—a senior employ who had been with the organization significantly longer than she—and said, "How does that comment fit into the Culture Brand we have here?" Of course, it didn't fit at all, and everyone knew it.

The business owner highlighted the importance of the Culture Brand during training, calling it part of their DNA. The new team member had bought into the idea and wanted to be a part of an organization with that positive culture. The anti-culture behavior of the middle manager clearly didn't align with what she had been promised.

I love that story because it shows the power of having a culture framework that is greater than the personalities in the business. I also love the fact that this brand-new team member was able to call *up* a team leader in a meaningful way, relying on the authority of the Culture Brand.

A Culture-Driven People Strategy

We cascade culture through organizations by integrating it into every aspect of the people strategy. I alluded to this early in the book and want to dive a little deeper into what this looks like and how it can work for your organization.

Hiring Guide

Hiring is one of the most powerful ways to put your Culture Brand to work. When you're clear on the culture you're building, you have a framework to evaluate candidates—not for perfection, but for alignment.

A strong hiring strategy evaluates behaviors and values by asking interview questions that go beyond skills and experience to target the key aspects of your culture—results, teaming, and character. With good questions, you can identify how closely someone aligns with your culture, where the gaps are, and whether they have the capacity to grow in the areas that matter most. The best candidates will be strong in at least two areas and willing to grow in the third. The goal isn't to find perfect people—it's to find individuals with strong character who will thrive and grow within your organization.

Take some time to evaluate your current hiring questions and compare them to your Culture Brand. Are they too weighted in one area? Are they missing key cultural traits? What questions do you need to add to ensure you are covering behaviors and attitudes related to results *and* teaming *and* character?

Role Clarity

Once you have a clear picture of the culture you're building, you can use that insight to define roles and job descriptions. With its three key areas of results, teaming, and character and the nine subcategories, you have a comprehensive framework to clarify roles in a way that reinforces your culture.

Results
- Goal-driven
- Pursues Excellence
- Holds Others Accountable

Teaming
- Collaborates
- Develops Others
- Encourages

Character
- Coachable
- Dependable
- Takes Ownership

By structuring roles around these nine areas, you create clarity at every level of the business. A new hire at the entry level needs to embody these traits at a foundational level. For example, dependability for them might mean showing up on time, meeting deadlines, and wearing the correct uniform. As someone moves up in the organization, that increased responsibility means that dependability takes on greater weight. In addition to the basic standards, like being on time, they are expected to be dependable with their attitude and emotions, in the way they present themselves to the rest of their team, and in doing what they say they are going to do.

This framework allows you to scale expectations appropriately. The same qualities exist at every level, but they evolve with responsibility. When writing job descriptions, this approach ensures you're defining roles not just by skills, but by the behaviors, emotional intelligence, and cultural alignment necessary for success.

Leadership Assessments

One of the biggest challenges in leadership evaluations is when a leader isn't performing at the necessary level, and their supervisor simply tells them, *"You need to grow your leadership"*—without offering specifics about what needs to change. Without clear direction, meaningful growth is difficult.

The Culture Brand framework allows leaders to identify with laser-focused precision which areas need development. As described in the previous chapter, starting with *self*-evaluation rather than beginning with supervisor-led evaluation is a powerful strategy for building awareness.

When a leader identifies their own gaps in performance and behavior, they're far more likely to take ownership of their growth and be receptive to feedback.

The Culture Brand self-assessment tool enables leaders to evaluate themselves and identify areas of strength and weakness. Then, with a peer or supervisor, they can share their self-evaluations, discuss their findings, and have a productive conversation that points to specific areas to focus on. This shifts the evaluation from a one-sided critique to a shared development process.

Some leaders question the effectiveness of a self-assessment, assuming that the person is unaware of their weaknesses or simply unwilling to change. You certainly can confront the problem head-on; however, we have found it's more effective to let the person discover and identify areas of weakness. Start with the areas they are willing to acknowledge and build from there. Over time, you earn the right to challenge their blind spots.

If there's a major disconnect—where a leader rates themselves much higher than you would—you have an opportunity for deeper discussion. A simple question like, *"I noticed you rated yourself an eight in this area—can you give me an example of when you demonstrated that?"* opens the door for clarity. It may just be a difference in how each person interprets the scale. What one person sees as a *five*, another may see as an *eight*. Talking through these differences helps align expectations and makes leadership evaluations far more productive.

Performance Reviews

Performance reviews tend to focus on measurable results areas and leave out character and teaming behaviors. Use your Culture Brand to balance out your review system by incorporating all three areas into performance expectations. With clear targets, you can create a rating system that shows growth over time. I also recommend using a survey that includes self-evaluation as well as a 360 assessment, a peer review using the same questions. This dual approach to performance evaluations quickly highlights areas of low awareness and provides healthy feedback. Conducting regular reviews and charting the ratings allows you to show change over time. Here is an example:

If you follow this plan, I recommend that the review include examples for each question that are relevant to each specific role and level of responsibility.

Take a look at your current performance review questions. Do they match with the results, teaming, and character expectations you've identified with your Culture Brand? Have you covered all three areas?

Create a Developmental Path

You probably have team members who want to reach for the next promotion. Your Culture Brand can be used to outline your career path to ensure success at each new level. Remember the ladder example from Chapter One? Promotions should take both sides of the growth ladder into consideration. With the Culture Brand firmly in place, you have an additional set of parameters to discuss with emerging leaders. They may have tenure, and they may have been able to prove their operational skill, but operational skill at one level will not guarantee their success in the next.

Use your Culture Brand to define the behaviors required for each level. Assign those clear behaviors to each role at each level. Take into account the subcategories of each of the three Culture Brand areas as a framework for more clearly describing the necessary behaviors. For example, for a team member who works in production, the responsibility to hold others accountable may be significantly more challenging at the next level of leadership.

If they have not had that responsibility before, they may struggle to hold others accountable. Your development path, in this example, should include training, evaluation, and coaching to ensure that team member exhibits the necessary skills *before* giving them the responsibility to hold an entire production line accountable to quality.

If someone on your team approaches you about growth, you are duty bound to help them have awareness about where they are currently on their journey and what next steps will be required. Too often, leaders rely on the sink-or-swim approach. Maybe they don't think they have time to invest in developing others, or they just don't know how. Integrating your Culture Brand into your coaching, training, and development saves you time and heartache by creating awareness about what is working, what isn't, and what is needed next.

Aligning all of your development courses around your culture does two things for your organization.

It strengthens your employee value proposition (EVP) by showcasing team member development. This branded approach highlights the uniqueness of the culture you are building.

Building the development system around Culture Brand allows you target specific strengths and weaknesses.

What Is an EVP?

An EVP is what employers can use to talk about the benefits of being employed by the organization. One of these can be personal development. This type of development is an investment in the employee's future, whether in this organization or elsewhere.

The key to development at every level is having a goal. Team members and emerging and established leaders can lean into their strengths, building on what they already do well, or they can focus on an area where they struggle and want to improve. Aligning your training with your Culture Brand ensures that everyone is growing in the right direction.

Exiting Team Members

This benefit was well-covered in the previous chapter as a benefit of Culture Brand. I won't expound on it here except to say that with a clear guide for behavior and the coaching and evaluation methods discussed thus far, leaders experience greater confidence when it becomes clear that it's time to let someone go. So often, I have leaders who deal with remorse about exiting a leader. They wonder if they were clear enough and supportive enough. Culture Brand gives you a method for being clear about behavior.

Give It Time

Creating a healthy culture takes time. Culture Brand, while simple and highly actionable, is not a quick fix. As we've seen, consistency of messaging and behavior—from the top down—is essential. Even so, some teams stall or have a slow start when implementing their Culture Brand. When that happens, it's usually for one of two reasons:

1. **The leader is not focused on culture.** When leaders are not committed and emotionally invested in developing a strong, culture-driven team, others feel it. The organizations that have benefited the most from Culture Brand are those where the top leadership relentlessly kept the message strong. They find ways to introduce their culture words into all communication. They share stories and celebrate team members who exemplify the culture ideals. If they do not, the team reverts to old thinking and believes the culture transformation initiative was another "flavor-of-the-month" idea.

2. **Culture change is hard.** It is a bit more like heart surgery than first aid. We are working to address attitudes and actions, and we are working to change long-standing habits. Some behaviors that have been allowed or tolerated are now being addressed. The Culture Brand only works if the leaders are willing to hold others accountable and be held accountable for the desired behaviors.

Small Goals Lead to Big Growth

Part of being a leader is seeing the big picture and setting longer-term goals. At the same time, we cannot lose sight of the responsibility to lead in the moment where growth is actually happening.

Integrating Culture Brand into your people strategy allows the opportunity for small wins to lead to big wins. Consider two of the systems that we have introduced so far, and let's put them together. An annual evaluation offers a macro view of growth. If that is your only process, the focus is on making big strides. By combining those evaluations with regular developmental coaching conversations, you help support your team members in their day-to-day growth. Micro growth contributes to macro growth, helping to ensure your team members' success.

Focus on One Area at a Time

One of the business owners we work with recently shared a best practice with me. He focuses on one element of his organization's Culture Brand every few weeks. Throughout the year, he cycles through each of the nine subcategories of their Culture Brand. Taking time to go deep into that actionable value, he highlights what it means for the organization and calls everyone up to that characteristic. Each time he has an opportunity to speak to a group within his team, he chooses a new subcategory and shares a story or explanation about why it is important to support the larger Culture Brand ideals.

Call to Action:
Do a SWOT analysis on your Culture Brand results.

One of my clients' organizations was a year into implementing its Culture Brand. The leadership team had noticed some changes, but because it can be difficult to see transformation as it happens, they did a SWOT analysis to evaluate progress on their culture journey.

It's a smart practice! Conducting an annual Culture Brand review can help you see where you're building momentum and where your team needs additional coaching or support.

Here's how to go about conducting your own SWOT analysis for your Culture Brand:

1. Gather any Culture Brand Assessment data, including reviews, stories, engagement surveys, and customer satisfaction surveys. You can add any other significant data to this body of information.

2. Examine this information through the lens of your Culture Brand. See if there are correlation points between your culture expectations and your results data.

3. Use the four questions of a SWOT analysis to organize your findings.

   • What are our strengths?

   • What are our weaknesses?

   • What are our opportunities?

   • What are our threats?

4. Create action plans to address all four areas, including leveraging strengths.

PART FOUR:
LEADERS SCALE CULTURE

We don't compromise on culture.

The merger was official by the first Monday in June.

The email announcement went out at 8:00 a.m. sharp: *Intelex welcomes the NovaTech team to our family.*

By 8:05, Kate's inbox was full.

The messages fell into two categories: excitement and panic.

NovaTech's people were warm and enthusiastic, eager to collaborate. Many signed off with phrases like, So glad to be part of the team! or Looking forward to meeting everyone soon!

Her Intelex leaders, on the other hand, sent notes laced with unease:

"Who's making final decisions now?"

"Do we have clarity on reporting structure?"

"Will this slow down our timelines?"

Kate had expected growing pains, but she hadn't anticipated how quickly the tension would surface.

The first joint leadership meeting was supposed to be a celebration. It felt more like a standoff.

The NovaTech leaders—bright, relational, and full of ideas—chatted easily among themselves, greeting everyone by name. The Intelex VPs were polite but guarded, leaning back in their chairs, arms crossed.

Culture Brand

Kate began with her best smile. "I want to start by saying how grateful I am for each of you. This merger is about combining strengths—NovaTech's innovation and customer focus with Intelex's scale and systems. Together, we can reach new markets in new ways."

Nods. Smiles. Even a little applause.

But as soon as the agenda turned tactical, the energy shifted.

NovaTech's VP of client experience, a woman named Ananya, suggested that the average project timeline be extended to improve customer satisfaction scores.

Ryan jumped in almost immediately. "That's not realistic. Our clients expect us to deliver fast. If you slow us down, we'll lose them."

Ananya met his gaze calmly. "I understand, but our retention rates speak for themselves. Maybe speed isn't the only metric that matters."

Silence fell on the room.

Kate interjected quickly. "Let's capture both perspectives. I think there's wisdom on both sides."

But she had already seen the glances and the whispered side comments. A quiet division was forming between "us" and "them."

By the end of the first week, the problems multiplied. NovaTech employees felt bulldozed. Intelex teams complained that their new counterparts were "too touchy-feely." An email thread about process updates spiraled into a twenty-six-message argument.

Then came the client call.

A longtime account—one of Intelex's top five—had worked with NovaTech before the merger. They called Kate directly, frustrated by contradictory messages from two account managers, one from each company.

"I don't care what your org chart looks like," the client said. "I just want one honest answer. I have to say, Kate, if this chaos is an indication of how things are changing, maybe we need to reevaluate our contract."

We don't compromise on culture.

That night, Kate sat in her darkened office long after everyone had gone home. The city's lights glowed below, but her thoughts darkened with doubts and frustration.

How did we get here so fast?

She picked up her phone and scrolled to Scott's name.

He answered on the second ring. "Hey there, CEO. How's the merger coming along?"

Kate laughed dryly. "Like merging a baseball team with a football team."

He chuckled. "That bad?"

"Worse. They're talking *about* each other instead of *to* each other. Neither respects the other. Yet. I'm trying to get everyone playing by the same rules, but they keep arguing about who's calling the shots and which playbook to use."

Scott was quiet for a long moment. Then he said, "Do you remember Clark's cotton field story?"

"Never blame the crop," she said automatically.

"That's right," he said. "Two different crops just got thrown together. It's your job now to make sure both have the soil they need to grow."

Kate sighed. "So more fertilizer?"

He laughed. "More truth. More time. More leadership."

The following week, she convened a joint team meeting in the company auditorium. She'd spent all weekend preparing, rewriting, and praying over her remarks.

When everyone had settled, she began.

"I know the last few weeks have been hard," she said. "We've had confusion, tension, even frustration. And I'll be honest—it's been hard for me too. We're learning how to be one company. That doesn't happen overnight."

She paused, letting the silence stretch.

Culture Brand

"But here's what I believe: We have to grow—together. If we're willing to do the work, we can create a business that's stronger than ever."

Her voice steadied. "At Intelex, we use three words to define the culture: Advance. Elevate. Trust. Those aren't just pretty words; they're who we are and the way we work. They apply to every person in this room—whether you've been part of the Intelex group for years or today is your first day as part of this company. We don't compromise on culture. With this merger, we've all gained a wealth of expertise. The way we do things may look and feel a little different. But what isn't changing is our culture. We Advance. We Elevate. We Trust.

"And because of that culture, I know that we can all learn from one another and find new and perhaps even better ways to live out those three words. We owe that to each other—and to all our clients."

Then she asked everyone to stand, find someone from the other company, and spend five minutes answering one question: What do you love most about how your team works?

At first, people hesitated. Then laughter began to ripple through the room. For the first time since the merger, she saw a spark of connection.

Later, as Kate packed up her notes, Ananya approached her.

"That was a good move," she said. "I think people needed permission to see the good in each other again."

Kate smiled, tired but encouraged. "I hope so. We've got a long road ahead."

Ananya hesitated, then said, "You know, one of your guys told me earlier today that he misses the 'old Intelex.' I told him that's okay. I miss the old NovaTech sometimes too. But maybe we're both supposed to learn from each other."

Kate nodded slowly. "I think we are."

We don't compromise on culture.

That night, she texted Scott:

> Small win today. Still a lot to do, but I think the crops are going to make it.

His reply came a minute later.

> Then keep tending it, farmer. Growth takes time.

Kate smiled. Maybe so. But it was good to see a hint of green breaking through the dirt.

Chapter 8
The Tipping Point

If you get the culture right, most of the other stuff will just take care of itself.

—Tony Hsieh

When the culture you've designed drives the mission forward without your daily intervention—*and* stays in alignment with your purpose and values on the path to the vision—you can breathe a deep sigh of relief. This is Culture Brand at work.

You can't build culture alone. By its very nature, culture requires community. Neither can you *scale* culture by yourself; healthy culture requires leadership. You may be the chief culture officer, but that doesn't mean you bear the sole responsibility for your culture. For your Culture Brand to permeate, unify, and drive your organization, you will need a team of culture leaders who know how to develop other leaders. The multiplication of leadership is essential not only for growing your organization but for doing so in a way that ensures its health.

A business owner I coach recently shared a story with me that demonstrates the real benefit of Culture Brand. He happened to walk in on a corrective conversation between a leader and a team member—only to find them pausing, searching for their laminated Culture Brand self-assessment. After a brief search and with the assessment tool finally in hand, the leader confidently and competently continued the conversation with the team member.

As the owner observed the interaction, he felt reassured. It was clear that this leader recognized the value of having a clear and actionable culture. In the past, the owner would have had to lead that kind of tough conversation. Now, his leadership team was confidently taking ownership because they had a clear framework to follow. It gave him confidence that his leaders were relying on the tool for consistency and clarity.

It also pleased the owner to see that one side of the assessment had their Culture Brand in English, the other in Spanish. Clarity is kind—not just for the person receiving feedback but for the leaders delivering it.

All the work of designing and aligning your culture up to this point has required a great deal of effort on your part as a leader. To build momentum and reach the tipping point, however, you can't be the only one driving culture.

Until you reach the tipping point, you may feel as if you are pushing against a giant boulder, trying to get it to start rolling. Depending on the starting point in terms of the health or dysfunction of your organization,

> **Clarity is kind—not just for the person receiving feedback but for the leaders delivering it.**

getting your leadership team on board with culture, proving how serious you are about the desired culture, and explaining its benefits might have felt like pushing that boulder *uphill*. Growing a healthy culture takes time and effort and lots of energy.

If you are persistent in the groundwork, however, culture-building won't seem nearly as heavy. When you develop a leadership team that is willing to work *with* you to design and implement your Culture Brand, that boulder will gather momentum. You'll notice, just like that business owner did, that things keep rolling with far less effort on your part because others are doing their part to maintain the forward movement. With consistency and care, everyone on the team will buy into the culture. This is the tipping point, and it's when things really start rolling!

Everyone wants to start here—where the momentum is in full force, things feel easy, and growth is exponential. But that's not how building a healthy culture works. You can't skip the earlier steps and get right to results.

The deliberate work you've done to get to this point laid the foundation for tangible, *visible* growth. The reality is, you were growing all along, even when the results weren't visible. Don't discount what you've done to build a scalable and sustainable structure. Take a moment to recognize how far you've come.

When you started this Culture Brand journey, you may have had many of the right pieces in place and some wonderful successes to celebrate. Now, however, I hope your confidence in your organization has increased exponentially as you've built something that is no longer completely dependent on you. With your simple, comprehensive culture design gaining traction, your leaders can scale their teams as personal and peer accountability grow.

It is so incredible when business owners and executives reach this tipping point. The confidence they have in their team is priceless. This becomes even more insightful as they look back at the time when the stress of managing every aspect of the organization overburdened them. In those stressful days, the future looked bleak because it seemed that the weight of carrying the organization would only increase as the business grew. Before clarifying the culture, their organization seemed fragile. They felt compelled to dig into each behavior issue. With good reason, they worried that there wouldn't be enough ownership of the tasks to keep the business running or that good people would walk out because of the toxic environment. Those are very real threats to any organization, and shifting to healthy culture doesn't immediately eliminate those risks. But it does minimize them.

When your new culture becomes nonnegotiable, there is a very real possibility that some people will leave. I've seen it happen several times. But every single time, there was a sense of progress toward team cohesiveness. When toxic behavior walks out the door, people rejoice.

Keys to Scaling Your Culture

Here are six tipping points to gain cultural momentum:

Multiply Leaders

With your framework and the culture alignment it promotes, it should be easier to identify those in your organization who build and protect healthy culture. Once you've identified these culture leaders, elevate them to their highest capability. Continue to coach and equip them with the tools and strategies to help them succeed. They will champion culture even when you are not looking and will expand the foundation of trust throughout your organization.

Multiply Momentum

Once you start gaining traction with culture alignment, you'll feel the momentum build. The cultural shifts that took so much effort to get moving will become more self-sustaining. Your role transitions from pushing to directing—less about getting things started and more about keeping everything aligned and moving toward the vision.

Pro Tip: Rescue less. One way to do this is to shift your thinking from commanding to curious. When you are commanding and directing, the team responds by doing rather than thinking. They continue to depend on you to do the thinking. When you shift to being curious and approaching situations with questions, the team will learn to think for themselves and try to anticipate your questions. They will start looking at situations from your perspective and examine the business from a higher business horizon. This shift in your leadership helps leaders win at the next tipping point.

Multiply Ownership

I have much to say on the topic of ownership that I don't have space here to unpack. (If you're curious, check out the workshop, coaching, and tools package I've developed called EveryLevel Ownership System™ at JayRaines. com/ELOS.) For this discussion, I want to pull just one thread that is fundamental to ownership topic: taking responsibility for personal growth.

We live in a blame culture, where it is often difficult to find people who take responsibility for their actions; in fact, it's so rare that leaders are actually surprised and delighted to find anyone with this level of personal responsibility. Fortunately, ownership can be developed and multiplied throughout your organization.

Fostering an environment that expects personal ownership begins with personal connection. Your Culture Brand is a tool for helping our team members take ownership of their performance and development. It starts by asking them to become more self-aware of how they interact with the world and people around them. Even as it communicates that you are all working toward a shared mission and vision, success will require their personal engagement. In other words, each person needs to know they matter to the team and that they play an important role.

The starting point of personal ownership is when a leader calls out someone's potential. It's very likely someone did this for you. They saw something in you that was greater than where you were at the time, and they called you up to a new view of yourself.

I have had many people throughout my life who have invested in me in this way. I would not have founded LeadersQ or written this book were it not for them. One person, in particular, comes to mind: Scott Clark. Several years ago, he sat me down and told me he believed I should start a company developing leaders—beginning with his.

You might have noticed that I've named two characters in this story after him. In many ways, I see my mentor and friend as *both* characters—a business leader who built a team and gave his best for his family, friends, brand, and organization and a wise sage who engaged with and poured into people just by being himself.

Scott passed away a few years ago after a sudden illness. Several thousand people attended his funeral, and everyone I spoke to that day said they felt as if Scott had treated them like their closest friend. I felt the same way. He was always so *present* with people. I hope to be that kind of friend to those around me. He saw something in me that I didn't see in myself, and I decided to believe what *he* believed about me.

The people whose lives you speak into will have the same choice. Some will rise to the challenge. Others won't. You can't control their response, but you can increase your impact by intentionally calling people up to their potential.

Multiply Confidence

I find that leaders are hesitant to act, not because they lack competence, but because they lack confidence. Culture Brand provides a guide for building confidence. Hubris and egotism are rampant in unhealthy cultures, but that's not the kind of confidence we're multiplying with Culture Brand; in fact, those are the kinds we're pruning. What we're growing with Culture Brand is grounded in the kind of healthy environment where people thrive. When we equip leaders and team members with a clear definition of healthy culture, it fosters confidence about promoting and protecting that culture. That confidence takes root first with the leadership team and then flourishes when those leaders are faithful to the Culture Brand they helped design. When everyone at every level is empowered to nurture and protect the culture, that confidence cascades through the entire organization.

Multiply Accountability

Accountability to the culture can move up and down the organization's ladder, and it can happen across the team meeting table. Lapses in culture are more quickly noticed and more accurately addressed with a clear, measurable cultural definition. Each person, regardless of position or role, can look at a situation and accurately pinpoint the failures in healthy behavior. Everyone has the opportunity and responsibility to own their role in a toxic interaction or missed opportunity.

Multiply Trust

Trust is the essential currency in the economy of a winning organization. If ownership, confidence, and accountability are truly scaling within an organization, there will be a correlating and palpable growth in trust. That increased trust also ensures the growth of personal ownership, confidence, and accountability. One begets the other, just as distrust breeds dysfunction.

> **Trust is the essential currency in the economy of a winning organization.**

Trust is more like an onion than a light switch. We tend to think of trust as either on or off, true or false, present or absent. The reality, however, is that trust is layered. Think of it this way. Think of one of your leaders and ask yourself a few questions:

- Do I trust this person to hold the keys to my car?
- Do I trust them to hold my wallet with cash in it?
- Do I trust them with my personal bank login information?

I would imagine that most of you would answer yes to the first two questions and no to the third. This is a typical response. The point of this exercise is to show that trust has depth. What we have to determine is how much trust you need to have to work with someone. Then we have to determine additional layers of trust needed as that person moves to higher positions in the organization. You may trust them to interact with a customer but not with the monthly financial statement's accuracy.

Culture Brand gives you a framework for identifying areas of trust and distrust. You can then provide opportunity for them and for you to practice building trust in each area. You may trust them to be excellent and, at the same time, doubt whether they will develop another leader around them.

Leadership Behaviors to Build and Maintain Culture Momentum

As these multiplications build momentum in your organization, I encourage you to continue to develop your skills as a culture leader. Keep these key principles in mind as you put focused energy into scaling culture and developing new culture leaders.

Lead with Vulnerability

When there are stumbles at the top, expose them. Admit them openly. Show your humanity and willingness to be accountable to the culture. The moment you start hiding cultural missteps, distrust takes hold. But if you will own up to behaviors that don't align with your culture—and correct them—you can leap forward toward increased organizational trust.

Celebrate Wins

Celebrate the wins and attach each win to one aspect of your Culture Brand. I call this "hashtagging" your Culture Brand. If your Culture Brand is *Aspire, Respect, Thrive*, and one of your leaders goes out of their way to invest in another team member, take their photo holding up a sign that says #Respect and celebrate their culture-building behavior. Consistently attach each celebration-worthy moment to an aspect of the culture you are building.

Continually Define the Culture

Keep defining the meaning of your Culture Brand. The celebration exercise above is one way to define your meaning, but it is also important to speak about these culture qualities on a regular basis.

One of the CEOs I coach uses their Culture Brand as a guide when planning events throughout the year. Every time the company welcomes a batch of new hires or holds a group celebration, he takes a few minutes to unpack one of the terms more deeply and elevate the importance and value of a single aspect.

We have worked hard to make it simple to clarify and share your Culture Brand. The danger in this simplicity is neglecting to dive into the depths of each concept. All aspects of leadership and growth fit into at least one of the three main areas of *results, teaming,* and *character.* That means the well of meaning for each one of the words you've chosen for your Culture Brand is deep! Be intentional about exploring these words with your team. Use your Culture Brand to ensure you devote time to each in your communication.

Measure Engagement

When there is a gap in organizational performance, use your Culture Brand to measure engagement. When someone on your team has serious gaps in the Culture Brand areas, it is a gap of engagement with the culture. Remember, when we develop our culture framework, we are communicating that this is the standard by which we try to show up at work and for the team. Where there is a serious and noticeable gap, the team feels it. It leads to disconnects and misunderstandings with coworkers and inadvertently communicates a lack of engagement on the part of the individual. Awareness, honestly, and accountability for each area are the path to higher engagement. What area most needs support, results, teaming, or character? Conduct a SWOT analysis or review your team members' assessments to see what might be lacking.

Pro Tip: Leverage technology.

Culture Brand 360: One of our teams turned their semi-annual review into a growth plan by mapping each review question to a specific Culture Brand competency. They identified four role-specific behaviors for Be (Character), Play (Teaming), and Win (Results). These questions were rated by the employee and also rated by three coworkers. The resulting data provided a picture of their growth over a period of time. It also showed gaps in self-perception vs. environment.

Nurture Your Culture

I'm a terrible gardener, but I know enough to know that it takes persistent care for there to be a return on the investment. Every seed planted has the potential for a high yield in return; likewise, every plant requires labor input in the form of watering, weeding, and ensuring the proper nutrients to protect the healthy growth of each plant. The garden's expansion depends on the available resources and reliability of the tools and systems in place for care and harvesting. If those resources are overextended or the tools or systems are inefficient, the quality and yield will decrease.

If organizational culture is like a garden, it's easy to see how technology can aid in scaling through communication and training. But technology, though helpful, can never fully replace the necessity of human involvement in nurturing culture.

Culture Brand provides the framework and system for guiding human behavior—from the leaders to team members to peers. But people need people. We need leaders who add empathy to conversations and inspiration in specific moments. We need leaders who will observe and respond when someone needs to be challenged or supported. Nurturing culture can't be outsourced to technology or systems.

Focus on Health

Spend less time on removing anti-mission behaviors and more time promoting and developing pro-mission behavior. Back to the gardening example, weeding is one of the most time-consuming aspects of gardening. That tedious task is all but eliminated when you use a ground cover that only leaves space for the desired plants to grow. In so many ways, Culture Brand provides that ground cover. It helps prevent negative behavior from ever taking root. Eliminate the distractions of culture-destroying behavior by getting super clear about the culture you want to build. Divisive and toxic cultures are a drain on essential resources. Maximize your finite resources by focusing on a multiplying, healthy culture.

Emphasize a Growth Mindset

Thrive. That's what we all want our organizations to do. Thriving begins with the individual. Thriving is the basis of all scale. If the individuals in your organization are thriving, the entire organization has a chance to thrive.

A growth mindset is a powerful key for unlocking potential. Reward your team members with encouragement and engagement around their individual growth. When each individual is moving toward personal growth, there will be organizational dividends.

Create a Development Path

Create clear developmental steps for members to grow in your organization. I discussed earlier how Culture Brand can be included in job descriptions for every level and every role of an organization, from top to bottom. Take time to differentiate each level and role with specific behavior expectations in each job or role description.

This leveled approach to Culture Brand behaviors maps to roles in the organization and opens the door for you to have a development path for everyone on your team. Remember the ladder of development illustration I shared in Chapter One? The two sides of a ladder work together to help people move up and through the levels of an organization. Success requires hard skills and cultural and emotional skills. Create a development path that ensures people have opportunities to develop both as they move forward. There is no healthy way to scale an organization without individual growth. Equipping emerging leaders with the resources they need to succeed in cultural and emotional intelligence not only allows them to be more successful but also fosters the health of your organization.

Lead Out Loud

Leading out loud is instrumental to transforming *and* scaling your culture. If you've done this from Day One of your Culture Brand design, your team will have observed your modeling along the way. Your best leaders emulate your behavior. If they have observed your process of coaching, challenging, defining, assessing, disciplining, etc., then they will be equipped to cascade this behavior and model for other emerging leaders. Keeping your processes and tools a mystery makes your emerging leaders dependent on you for handling sticky situations.

Share Your Transformation Story

Stories have emotional and educational value that can be leveraged to scale culture. They are effective because we are wired for story. Humanity has millennia of culture developed around storytelling.

> You can't have culture without story.

You can't have culture without story. It is the thing that makes culture tangible and shareable. Story is how we perpetuate and scale culture. It's so important that our team at LeadersQ has coaching specifically designed to help leaders develop and leverage storytelling techniques.

Stories have a way of communicating so much more than a training or slide deck could ever deliver. Here are a few story principles to follow as you develop your story-curation skills:

- **Choose a person.** People empathize better with a person than a group. Tell the story of a person and how they displayed the value that you want to highlight.
- **Add emotion.** Find ways to show struggle and triumph in your story.
- **Show the journey.** Bring the listener into the journey and allow them to participate in the triumph by painting the scene and coloring it with authentic emotion.
- **Use stories in multiple venues.** Use a story for orientation, training, highlighting positive behavior, and team meetings. Stories help bring your culture to life. Have a story ready for every communication avenue in the organization.

Pro Tip: Use the STAR method for story crafting. One simple method for crafting a story is to take time to describe each of these story parts: Situation, Trouble, Action, Result. Use these questions to guide your story:

What was the situation? "So there we were . . ."

What was the trouble that we faced? "We wanted to, but . . ."

What steps or actions did you take? "So we . . ."

What happened as a result of your action? "So then we (found, saw, realized) . . . ."

My hope is that, in time, you will tell your story of transformation beyond the walls of your organization. You have a story to tell that is inspiring for others. You learned to lead your organization and capture the heart of your team. You learned to do something greater than what you could have done with a disjointed culture. The world needs to hear stories like that. The world needs to see that we can unify and win together, achieving a shared vision.

Call to Action: Establish a Leadership Development Plan

Evaluate your leadership development courses and identify which of the three Culture Brand categories each one addresses. Notice if there is a balance in training for both sides of the ladder of development. If there are gaps, fill them. Take this a step further and consider the nine subcategories listed in Chapter Four. Consider adding more training around any of these areas that are missing or underserved in your training plan.

Next-Level Leadership: After you have a comprehensive leadership development plan, expand its efficacy by adding three developmental levels. Here are some suggested levels:

1. Self-Leadership (character)
2. Leading Teams (teaming)
3. Leading Organizations (results)

Or here is another approach:

Basic Leadership—Take a deep dive into your Culture Brand by examining all nine subcategories. Introduce basic leadership and emotional intelligence skills. Goal: Lead self and taking personal ownership of growth.

Emerging Leaders—Build upon the basic training with new skills to help emerging leaders face the increased responsibilities for their role. Skill development might focus on conflict resolution or detailed goal-setting. Goal: Lead others and personal ownership of a business area.

Advanced Leadership—Build upon the two earlier trainings with additional training around leading through others. This would include casting vision and managing layers of accountability. Goal: Develop leaders who lead others.

Culture isn't complete until everyone owns it.

Eleven months after the merger, the company felt different. Better in many ways. Stronger, more stable, but still not whole.

There were moments of real progress: cross-department teams celebrating joint wins, customers praising the improved service, and employee surveys showing higher trust. But under the surface, Kate sensed pockets of resistance—small, quiet corners where people still clung to the past.

The board was pleased with the numbers, but Kate knew numbers didn't tell the full story.

Culture isn't complete until everyone owns it.

That thought echoed in her mind as she prepared for the company's first national leadership conference.

Two hundred leaders from across divisions and time zones were flying in. It would be the first time the combined organization gathered as one.

She wanted it to matter.

The ballroom was massive, filled with round tables draped in navy linens. A massive screen at the front displayed the new company logo—an elegant blend of Intelex blue and NovaTech silver.

Culture Brand

Kate stood behind the curtain backstage, listening to the low buzz of conversation. Her heartbeat thudded in her ears.

Scott had texted her early that morning:

> Remember, leaders don't give speeches—they tell the truth.

She smiled at the reminder and stepped up to the lectern.

"Good morning," she began, her voice steady. "A year ago, two companies became one. And like any family, the blending hasn't always been easy. We've felt the growing pains. Had a few misunderstandings. Even some disagreements that got a little . . . spirited."

Laughter rippled through the room.

"But we've also had incredible wins. We've launched new products, gained market share, and improved customer satisfaction across the board. Those are achievements worth celebrating."

Applause erupted. Kate held up a hand to quiet the crowd. "But our numbers aren't the only thing that makes me proud. What I'm most proud of is the progress we've made in becoming a team."

Her tone softened. "I know this merger asked a lot from each of you. Some of you came from Intelex's fast-paced world of metrics and goals. Others from NovaTech's high-touch, service-centered culture. Both are valuable—but neither can carry us forward alone."

She clicked to the next slide: three words filled the screen. *Advance. Elevate. Trust.*

"These three ideas define our Culture Brand. They describe how we win—what we expect of each other, and what others can expect from us. But for this to work, it can't just be words on a wall. It has to live in our actions, every day."

She paused, then said, "Let me tell you a story about a tree."

"In my former role, I served on a team in India. While I was there, I got to visit the Great Banyan in Bengaluru (Bangalore). It's a living

Culture isn't complete until everyone owns it.

landmark that's at least 250 years old. Aside from its age and incredible size, what makes the Great Banyan remarkable is how it grows. The tree sends down roots from its branches. Those roots reach the ground, take hold, and become new trunks. Over time, it stopped looking like a single tree and started looking like a forest.

"The Great Banyan has survived cyclones and massive storms that broke major limbs. In fact, its original central trunk was lost one hundred years ago. And yet, the tree keeps growing. Today, its crown stretches nearly 1,600 feet around, rising about eighty feet high, covering almost five acres. It thrives because its strength is distributed. Its life continues because its roots keep creating new life.

"That's the legacy we're building. Our culture can't depend on one office, one product, or one personality. Advance, Elevate, Trust has to become the roots—behaviors that reach down, take hold, and stand up as new trunks in every team, city, and market we enter. Storms will come—mergers, markets, mistakes. We may lose a branch. We may even outgrow the original 'trunk' that started it all. But if we keep putting down roots—clear expectations, shared language, aligned behaviors—we'll look less like a single organization and more like a living network. We won't just survive change—we'll spread because of it."

She glanced across the room. "That's legacy. That's what we're doing here."

Kate drew a breath. "Which brings me to something important. I've realized that culture isn't something we can half-commit to. We can't say one thing and do another. We can't celebrate values we don't live by. So today, I want to draw a clear line."

She glanced toward the back, where Bill Sanders and several board members stood, arms crossed, watching. Then she looked back to the room.

"If this Culture Brand—the way we work together, lead together, and win together—doesn't align with what you want, that's okay. But this is your moment to decide. Because from this point forward, we're all-in. If this culture isn't for you, this is your moment to step away. If it is, then commit fully. Get in—or get out."

Silence fell on the room.

For a long moment, no one moved. Then someone began to clap. Another joined in. Soon, the room thundered with applause.

Kate felt the tension in her chest break—not from triumph, but from relief.

After the session, leaders approached her in clusters. Some thanked her. Some admitted they'd been skeptical but were ready to recommit.

Later that afternoon, as she stepped outside to catch her breath, she spotted a familiar face waiting near the hotel's café terrace.

"Didn't expect to see you here," she said, smiling as Scott handed her a cup of coffee.

"I figured you'd need this," he said. "And I wanted to see how it went."

Kate exhaled. "They stayed. Every single one of them."

Scott grinned. "That's because you didn't just tell them what culture is. You showed them what it looks like to root it—and replicate it."

She took a long sip of coffee, letting the warmth settle her nerves. "I was terrified."

"Good," he said. "That means it mattered."

That night, as the conference dinner wrapped up, Kate stood near the edge of the ballroom watching her people laugh and talk—her team.

Different accents, different backgrounds, different styles—yet one unified rhythm.

She thought of Clark's line Scott had shared—steady and sure: Great crops come from great soil.

For the first time, she believed the soil—and the roots—were ready for anything.

Chapter 9
Replicating Culture

A company's culture is the foundation
for future innovation.
—Brian Chesky

A dear friend and client of mine owns two franchise locations in a national brand. We have worked very hard with their team to help them establish a strong, healthy culture, and they have enjoyed enormous success and growth as a result of their efforts. One day, I was talking with the company's director of talent about the relationship between the two locations. They are just a few miles apart, and I wondered how they were similar—and different. The description she gave stuck with me. She told me they were a lot like siblings. These locations are in the same enterprise family and share an organizational culture, but because each location has different personalities in leadership, each has distinct traits within that enterprise family.

In the previous chapter, we looked at what it takes to scale culture within an organization. In this chapter, I want to address applications for replicating your entire organization. Our team has had the privilege of working with more than twenty organizations that have made the transition from single-location organizations to enterprises with multiple locations. As with the client company I mentioned above, replicating culture requires continuity from one location to the next while allowing for a degree of individuality in each one.

I should note from the outset that there could be situations where replicating culture may not be the best option. It seems to me, however, that those instances are infrequent. The exception to the rule would be if you own two or more organizations with very different contexts or missions. Under those circumstances, you might opt to design unique Culture Brands for each one.

Most of our clients are not launching completely distinct organizations. Rather, they are expanding locations, adding departments, or merging businesses. By the time they reach this level of organizational growth, their Culture Brand has become so much a part of their identity that the idea of changing it or starting over from scratch is almost unthinkable. It is also unnecessary. Their Culture Brand is part of the DNA that has fueled their success. It makes far more sense to build on it than to begin again.

Three Heroes

My company has had the privilege of working with more than eighty-plus Chick-fil-A owner-operators across the nation. Through monthly group training with teams, as well as individual executive leader coaching sessions, we have implemented, tested, and honed the Culture Brand concepts. As I learn more about this company, I have developed my own story about its brand, which is a great way to evaluate healthy scaling. I call it the "Three Heroes Story." It goes something like this:

Hero #1: Product

In 1964, Truett Cathy created what is now known simply as "the original chicken sandwich." That sandwich became the hero product for the Chick-fil-A enterprise that he started with his family. For many years, this product has been the central hero of the organization. It still holds the number-one spot on the menu and is the most recognizable product described on the website as:

"Our original recipe for almost sixty years. A boneless breast of chicken seasoned to perfection, freshly breaded, pressure-cooked in 100 percent refined peanut oil and served on a toasted, buttery bun with dill pickle chips."

Truett was relentless about quality in their expanding organization. The product had to have integrity across the chain. Accountability for that product is still extremely high. The hero has to be protected to remain consistent.

Hero #2: People

As the organization grew, another type of hero began to emerge: *people*. Truett, himself, was given hero status with his wise leadership and business savvy. Along the way, other heroes were identified:

- Jimmy Collins, the executive vice president, who for many years led the company through significant growth and major transitions, including moving into freestanding locations.
- Individual owner–operators who had outstanding accomplishments and innovations, like my friend Jerald Huggins, who started the movement away from talk-boxes in the drive-thru with some cell phones and a legal pad for ordering and changed the drive-thru experience forever. Or Bruce Ploeser, who started the First 100 the night before his Chick-fil-A Goodyear grand opening in Phoenix, Arizona, where those camping out could receive free food prizes.
- Outstanding team members who consistently made the best biscuits, the most perfect waffle fries, or changed a flat tire for a distressed customer.

These heroes, along with other shining stars who helped push the brand forward, were celebrated. The organization has long evaluated each individual restaurant's leadership team as important as its operational excellence. The corporate office expected to see both of these types of heroes, product and people, before granting any new opportunity.

Hero #3: Processes

In recent years, a new hero has risen to the top of evaluating each location: hero *processes*. The organization's corporate leadership has realized that the success of a local franchisee depends upon the quality of its systems and processes. These hero processes create dependable systems that do not depend solely on hero individuals and protect the hero products.

What stands out to me, as an observer on the outside looking in, is that Chick-fil-A Incorporated has more confidence in franchises that have strong systems led by winning leaders that deliver the highest quality in their product.

The best owner–operators in Chick-fil-A understand this need for all three heroes in their organization: Product, People, and Processes. Our work with many of these leaders has focused on helping them reach this "three-hero level" by developing both sides of the leadership ladder described earlier. On each side of the ladder, we help leaders develop people who deliver a hero product. At the same time, we provide a complete hero-building process—strengthening leaders on the culture and emotional intelligence side while also building execution, skills, and ownership on the right side of the ladder. This approach to talent development has become something teams celebrate. Because systems are reproducible, this system consistently develops more hero people while sustaining and protecting the hero product.

In Chick-fil-A's world, success demands all three. The company couldn't have grown to the size it has or established its reputation as a leader in customer service in this industry had it relied exclusively on just one of those heroes. The product has to be consistent across the nation and around the world. The processes ensure that consistency. The one wild card factor—the one thing that can't be replicated—is people. And that's where Culture Brand comes in to support the leaders we work with who want to expand to multiple locations—whether they're with this brand or any other.

Benefits of a Replicable People Strategy

The beautiful thing about people is that each one is unique. You, as the leader, are unique. You can't be duplicated. Nor can you be everywhere at once. That's the reason for designing your Culture Brand in the first place. Culture overrides personality. It overrides personal preferences. Culture guides. It drives. And if anything or anyone other than culture takes precedence, the road can get rocky.

Replicating Culture

The good news is that although people can't be replicated, processes can, which means your culture can be replicated. What I aim to give my clients and what I am now sharing with you is a way to build a replicable and dependable people system. Culture Brand enables you to protect the mission from the danger of mission drift, no matter how many locations, departments, or offices you have.

If you are an owner or the CEO who wants to expand your business, your role must change. In this move toward replication, you will experience some significant enterprise wins, but there are also some significant personal losses, namely control. You cannot lead today like you did yesterday. Each new enterprise will require that you become more distant from the front line of the mission. Depending on your personality, that may sound fantastic or terrifying. Regardless, you will be forced, more than ever, to lead through your leaders and trust them to make decisions in alignment with the PV^2M and your Culture Brand.

This is why I advocate the mental shift from CEO to CCO (chief culture officer). If you measure your successes around culture, you have much more opportunity to win and avoid getting pulled into decisions that should be made by others. At this level of scale, execution should be less dependent on you. In order for your leaders to lead at a higher level, you have to find ways to stay out of their way and keep pointing the way. Your Culture Brand helps keep everyone moving forward in the same direction. Here are a few more benefits of focusing on having a replicable culture:

A strong Culture Brand has a decentralized culture. When culture cascades through an organization, that momentum shifts into overdrive when you expand. At this stage of maturity, the majority of your team members perpetuate and protect the culture driving the mission. To put it into pilot terms, you are flying the plane with your fingertips rather than gripping the yoke. Any adjustments are minor, and most of the movement is in the right direction.

Culture Brand

A strong Culture Brand provides a more consistent customer experience. The end user of your brand is getting a more consistent interaction with your team members across the organization. They see a consistent engagement on your teams. Your people become your brand ambassadors with their behavior. Your customers learn to trust your teams to deliver. They will be surprised when there is a miss and more easily recovered when you work to reengage them.

A strong Culture Brand will have contagious hot coals. Starting a campfire is very challenging. It takes a lot of practice and many failures to get a blazing fire going. But if you could borrow a burning coal from someone else's fire, it could make the process go much faster. In organizations, people who are well-versed in and devoted to your Culture Brand are like those hot coals. They can help you more quickly spread your culture to another area of the business. They are culture leaders—regardless of their role or title. Some of our clients have taken on established organizations either as an owner relocation or as an acquisition. When you have a strong original culture, you can use some of those "hot coals" from that culture to ignite a new culture in the acquired organization. This takes time, but these hot coals do not have to be trained, and they can help accelerate the culture transformation that you need to happen in the new location. This can also be true of an entirely new location where there is a significant number of new hires. You can bring some strong culture leaders from the established location to encourage the expansion of culture in the new one.

A strong Culture Brand frees you from being the "fixer." When you have established your culture, you aren't left on your own to be the one who solves every problem and handles every emergency. The larger your organization grows, the more impossible it becomes to take on the role of the rescuer. It is also counterproductive because you undermine your leaders' authority every time you jump in and take over. It may feel rewarding to be the one with all the answers, but it can damage the trust you've worked so hard to build.

That said, you can be the model anytime. Jump in here and there to help out. Just be mindful of how often this occurs. Count how many times a week or a month you jump in. Ask yourself: "Was I modeling or rescuing?" Take the number of times you rescued and reduce that by half, then half again, until you are no longer expected to run in and save the day. If you are a known rescuer, your team might feel abandoned if you stop cold turkey. So find a way to reduce your emergency response syndrome, for your sake and for theirs.

A strong Culture Brand helps you create margin in your life. Stress is pervasive in our society, and for leaders in an unhealthy culture, it can be debilitating. One of the benefits of a strong Culture Brand is that it enables leaders to take a break from the stress of running their businesses. Some leaders initially have real difficulty stepping back and letting their leaders lead. The reason: a lack of trust. If leaders are unable to trust their leaders, they are less able to engage with culture and vision, and both will be lost.

The solution is to increase their leaders' ownership of responsibility in the business. When business leaders can trust the people leading the team to keep the mission on target, they can relax more in their daily lives. It frees them to engage in the culture today and the vision for tomorrow. True rest is in true trust.

> **True rest is in true trust.**

Call to Action: Build Your Culture to Scale

What would you duplicate if you could? If you had the opportunity to copy and paste your organization and replicate your culture, what would you keep? What would you eliminate?

This final step in the Culture Brand process, replicating culture at scale, challenges the best of leaders. Doing it successfully requires strengthening the first entity before launching the second. Don't wait. And don't fall into the trap of believing that you can "fix" things by starting fresh at the new location. The new location will need the best of you, and the reality is that you'll likely end up taking the old problems with you to the new location. Then you'll have two locations with unhealthy cultures and not enough time or energy to go around.

Regardless of whether you are ready to expand, take stock of your systems and resources.

- Do you have the people, strategy, and processes in place to ensure everyone's success?

- Is your current culture too people-dependent to replicate? Too reliant on you?

- What processes need to be easily replicated or transferred? Create a library of your systems—not just a binder with a few sheets of instructions, but a library that you would be proud to show to another business owner. The people you lead deserve that level of quality and clarity.

- Think long term. What changes would you need to make to your processes to multiply the value of your business to a buyer?

The point of this exercise isn't to open a new location, department, or region next week, next month, or next year. It is to prepare your organization to be its best now for you and for the people you're leading. Healthy, strong, vibrant cultures are easier to replicate, in large part because people want to be part of them. That's something you can build now with your Culture Brand.

Lead with Culture

In the story woven throughout this book, Clark is the wise father-in-law who inspires Scott. Clark's wisdom is an overflow of his lifestyle and his philosophy about how the world works. In that respect, he offers us all something to aspire to as we lead with culture. Certainly, we must be intentional about developing people and building strong organizations, but there should also be some natural, collateral impact.

When we design, align, scale, and even replicate our cultures, what we ultimately create is a leadership development engine. People in our care will flourish, collaborate, challenge, and grow in the best environment we can provide.

My paternal grandfather was my inspiration for Clark. I spent summer after summer with him on the West Texas cotton farm that he developed and nurtured his whole life. One of my most vivid memories is seeing him get out of his GMC truck at the edge of a field and walk between the rows of growing cotton. After about forty steps into the field, he would kneel down and examine one of the plants. Taking out his yellow-handled Case knife, he would cut off one of the young cotton bolls. Then, he cut that boll in half to get a closer look at how the plant was growing.

I learned so much from that one act that my grandfather repeated each growing season—for years.

He taught me it was his responsibility to care for the crop.

He showed me that caring for the crop meant inspecting the fruit, looking for disease and invasive pests.

He helped me understand that his responsibility didn't end with selecting good seed. A bountiful crop required regular attention and the proper conditions so that the seeds had the best chance to grow.

It was only one plant of thousands in that row of cotton, and it was one row in thousands in that field, and that was only one of his fields. But his care for that one plant reflected the way he cared for his entire cotton farming operation.

He planted his first crop shortly after World War II. Starting with a single field, he learned what was necessary to care for and expand the crop. Over the years, he leveraged technology to grow and care for more rows. By the time he retired from farming, he had faithfully grown his cotton operation from a handful of acres to a farm that went for miles. But in all of that growth, he never lost sight of the need to care for one plant, in one row that West Texas afternoon.

I learned it by accident because his care flowed out of who he was.

Your people will learn culture in much the same way.

Epilogue:
Leadership isn't about perfection.
It is about cultivation.

The morning sun poured through the floor-to-ceiling windows of Kate's office, painting the city in gold. She took a moment to savor her morning coffee, watching people hurry along the sidewalks below. The movement and purpose were a living picture of what her company had become.

Intelex was no longer divided or uncertain. It was alive—one culture, one team.

The first annual report since the merger showed that revenue was up, client satisfaction was at an all-time high, and employee engagement was soaring. The board had rewarded her with a bonus, and Bill Sanders sent a note of congratulations: "You've done more than steady the ship. You've changed the current."

But what meant more to her than any of that was the quiet confidence she felt when she walked the halls. Conversations hummed with collaboration instead of complaint. Teams celebrated each other's wins. Leadership meetings were no longer battlegrounds; they were problem-solving sessions filled with trust and laughter.

Culture Brand

Advance, Elevate, Trust wasn't an initiative. It was their culture. Their identity.

Two weeks earlier, an email from *Business Monthly* had landed in her inbox with the subject line:

Congratulations—Intelex Named One of the Best Places to Work.

The article praised the company's "clear sense of purpose, collaborative spirit, and values-driven leadership." Reading it brought tears to Kate's eyes—not because of the recognition itself, but because every word in that article had once felt impossible.

Her team framed the magazine cover and hung it in the lobby— right below the mission statement.

It was proof: the soil was good, and the harvest was real.

That same week, her inbox filled again—this time with invitations. Conference organizers from across the country wanted her to speak about Intelex's transformation. *How do you build culture that lasts? How did you align two companies after a merger? How do you get results without losing your people?*

At first, she hesitated—public speaking had never been her goal. But as she looked around at what her team had built, she realized she wasn't being asked to talk about theory. She was being asked to share a living story—one that might help other leaders cultivate what she'd learned: that culture isn't managed; it's multiplied.

Then came the phone call.

"Kate," said the voice on the line, smooth and confident. "I'm Mark Eddington, CEO of Meridian Industries. We've followed your work at Intelex with great interest. We're preparing for a major global expansion, and we'd love for you to lead it."

She was stunned. Meridian was three times the size of Intelex—a powerhouse known for aggressive growth but struggling with high turnover and low morale.

Epilogue

Mark continued, "We need someone who knows how to build culture. Someone who's proven it can be done."

Kate promised to think about it.

That night, she sat on her patio, weighing the offer. Part of her was flattered, even thrilled. It was the kind of opportunity that used to define success for her. But another part of her hesitated. She had built something special here. Could she really walk away now?

The next morning, she met with the Intelex board. After the usual financial updates and future projections, Bill spoke up.

"Kate, before we adjourn, there's one more item." He glanced around the table, then back at her. "We know other companies are calling. Frankly, they should be. What you've accomplished here has set a new standard for leadership."

Kate smiled politely, unsure where he was going.

Bill continued, "We don't want to lose you. The board has unanimously agreed to offer you a new role—President of International Operations. We're expanding into Europe and Asia next year. We want you to lead it."

For a moment, she was speechless.

He smiled. "You built a culture that works. Now we need you to scale it."

Kate exhaled, the weight of the moment settling in. "Thank you," she said quietly. "I'd be honored."

That afternoon, she drove across town to meet Scott. The Coffee Nook had expanded to a second location, just a few blocks away from the original. She smiled as she parked, remembering that first rainy afternoon she'd stumbled through his doors—tired, soaked, and desperate for hope.

Inside, the air smelled of roasted beans and cinnamon. Scott waved from behind the counter, apron dusted with espresso grounds.

"Still hands-on, I see," she teased.

He grinned. "Old habits. Besides, I like staying close to the soil."

Kate laughed. "Of course you do."

They found a corner table, the same kind of small, round table where their conversations had begun two years earlier.

"So," he said, leaning back. "How's the farm?"

Kate smiled. "Thriving. We just made Best Places to Work. And I got offered a job with another company."

Scott raised an eyebrow. "You're leaving?"

She shook her head. "No. The board offered me something even better—global head of operations for our international division. We're expanding overseas. I get to build the next chapter of our culture from the ground up."

He nodded and smiled. "You've become what you were looking for."

Kate's eyes softened. "I learned from good teachers."

They sat in comfortable silence for a moment. Then Scott gestured toward the window, where young baristas were setting out a new display.

"You see them?" he said. "That's my favorite part. They've taken ownership of this place. I barely have to give direction anymore—they are the culture."

Kate nodded. "That's what I want for Intelex. A culture that doesn't depend on me to survive."

"Sounds like you've built that," he said.

She looked down at her cup, tracing the rim with her finger. "We've built it," she corrected. "You, Clark, the people who taught me what culture really means."

Scott smiled. "Then you're ready for whatever comes next."

Kate leaned back, letting the weight of the moment settle. "I am. For the first time, I really am."

That evening, after leaving the coffee shop, Kate thought about the journey—the fear, the failure, the breakthroughs, the courage

it took to keep digging when the soil seemed too dry to grow anything at all. She realized something simple and profound: Leadership
wasn't about perfection. It was about cultivation.

As she reached her car, her phone buzzed—a message from her
new international director, checking in about the upcoming expansion plans.

She smiled as she typed back:

> "Let's build this right. Design it, align it, and scale it."

She slid her phone into her bag, started the engine, and glanced
once more at the city lights spreading before her like rows of illumi-
nated fields.

The harvest ahead was unknown—but she was ready for it.

Appendix: Word List

This is a small collection of words that have appeared in various workshops over the years. It is not an exhaustive list, but it serves as a place to prompt your own amazing ideas. We do not recommend starting from this list. Follow the steps in Chapter 5 to capture the most natural ideas with your team. Notice how some words work in more than one category.

Results	Teaming	Character
Consistent	Serve	Positive
Commit	Encourage	Invest
Excellence	Trust	Servanthood / Serve
Aspiring / Aspire	Commitment	Ownership / Own
Goal-oriented	Family	Humble
Act	Uplifting	Dependable
Innovative	Grace	Patience
Grow	Believe the best	Responsibility
Growth-Mindset	Assume the best	Transparency
Urgency	Generous	Care
Professionalism	Sharing / Share	Honesty
Craft	Unified	Trustworthy
Foresight	Together	Diligent
Framework	Diversity	True / Truth
Cutting Edge	Build	Believe
Emerge	Better together	Heart
Knowledge	Sharpen	Fidelity
Sight / insight / see	Partner / Partnership	Optimism
Responsive / Respond	Sow / Sowing	Grateful
Excellence	Cultivate / Nurture	Thankful
Stretch	Improve/ Hone	Present / Presence
Craft	Inspire	Authentic
Challenge	Challenge	Honest / Real
Clear	Invest	Empathetic
Focus		Curious
		Learner
		Moldable
		Ally
		Confidant

For Further Reading

Story Dash by David Hutchens

The Ideal Team Player by Patrick Lencioni

Culture Rules by Mark Miller

Leadership Is Language by L. David Marquet

Thanks for the Feedback by Douglas Stone, Sheila Heen

Multipliers: How the Best Leaders Make Everyone Smarter by Liz Wiseman

Bibliography

Cherng, Andrew and Peggy. "Andrew and Peggy's Deeply Held Values." Panda Expressed Podcast, Episode 20. August 19, 2019. https://www.panda-expressed.com/episode/20/andrew-and-peggys-deeply-held-values.

Chick-fil-A. "Chick-fil-A Chicken Sandwich." Chick-fil-A.com. https://www.chick-fil-a.com/menu/entrees/chick-fil-a-chicken-sandwich.

Collins, Jim, and Jerry I. Porras. *Built to Last: Successful Habits of Visionary Companies.* Random House Business Books, 2005.

Hyatt, Michael. *Your Best Year Ever: A Five-Step Plan for Achieving Your Most Important Goals.* Embassy Books, 2019.

Lencioni, Patrick M. *The Ideal Team Player: How to Recognize and Cultivate the Three Essential Virtues.* John Wiley & Sons, 2016.

Miller, Mark. *Culture Rules: The Leader's Guide to Creating the Ultimate Competitive Advantage.* Matt Holt, 2023.

Ries, Eric. *Lean Startup: How Today's Entrepreneurs Use Continuous Innovation to Create Radically Successful Businesses.* Currency, 2011.

Work with Us

Take the Next Step Toward Building Your Winning Culture Brand

When you are ready to design *your* Culture Brand, LeadersQ can help you move from insight to execution. Through coaching, workshops, and leadership development, Jay Raines and the LeadersQ team partner with you to build a culture that aligns your team around behaviors that drive results.

Learn more at **JayRaines.com**.

Bring *Culture Brand* to Your Team

Culture Brand is a powerful resource for leadership teams, managers, and organizations committed to building a strong, scalable culture. Volume discounts and additional resources are available when you purchase *Culture Brand* for your team, company, or professional association.

Connect with Jay Raines for Leadership Coaching, Speaking Engagements, and Workshops

With practical business insights and an engaging storytelling style, Jay equips audiences with actionable strategies and tools for immediate implementation. He tailors his message to resonate with each audience, from C-suite executives to frontline managers, and offers workshops as well as monthly group and individual coaching packages.

Topics include . . .
- An Introduction to the Culture Brand Framework
- Building a Culture Brand that Scales
- Aligning Leadership, Values, and Performance
- Designing Systems That Support Growth
- Culture as a Competitive Advantage

Connect with Dr. Jay Raines
- JayRaines.com
- LeadersQ Podcast
- linkedin.com/in/drjayraines

Acknowledgments

I am deeply grateful for those who have invested in me to help me grow as a person and a leader.

To my grandfathers, one a cotton farmer and one a welder turned preacher: may I live to be half the man each of you were.

To my parents: as I stood on your shoulders, you encouraged me and helped me shape my purpose as I launched into this big world.

To my bride, who always believes in me long before I can: Thank you for saying, "Go for it!" You are the greatest love of my life. The best is yet to come.

To all our kids (J & K, M), who have always embraced the adventure: I'm so proud of you. You are a gift beyond measure. You have helped bring this work to life.

To business owners and leaders we have coached: This work was born from doing life and work with you. You are all woven into these pages.

To our LeadersQ team of executive coaches: we have a great culture together and it is a joy to serve our clients with you.

To my client care team at LeadersQ: nothing really happens without your support and attention to detail.

To Erin Casey, my book coach and editor, along with her team at My Writers' Connection, for your guidance and creativity; Danette High for all the help and review edits; and Keri Burwell for that amazing writing concept that I needed: thank you all for helping me create this work.

Most highly, this book is dedicated to my Savior, who is the only one who can truly change the heart.

"For we are God's masterpiece. He has created us anew in Christ Jesus, so we can do the good things he planned for us long ago." —Paul, Ephesians 2:10, NLT

About the Author

Dr. Jay Raines is a leadership consultant and trainer with more than thirty years of experience. As the CEO and founder of LeadersQ, he comes alongside leaders, founders, and franchise owners to design cultures that move their mission forward and enable their organizations to scale with clarity and consistency.

Drawing on his experience working with a wide range of clients, including Chick-fil-A franchise owner–operators, biotech leaders, banking and accounting firms, real estate and home building companies, academic and nonprofit organizations, Jay brings clarity to the often intangible work of culture.

Prior to launching LeadersQ, Jay cofounded a leadership consulting company in India, where he worked with global clients such as Moog, Toyota, and UST Global. Jay's international perspective and varied real-world experience allow him to connect with leaders at every level across diverse industries. Whether he is presenting in a boardroom for a Fortune 500 company or delivering a workshop to frontline managers, his message equips leaders to transform workplace culture so that people and performance thrive together.

Known for his engaging and practical approach, Jay combines business insight with compelling storytelling, ensuring audiences leave with actionable strategies they can implement immediately.

When he isn't meeting with clients or recording the LeadersQ Podcast, Jay enjoys fly fishing, camping with his wife, gardening, and roasting coffee in pursuit of the perfect cup.

Connect with Jay at JayRaines.com.

www.ingramcontent.com/pod-product-compliance
Lightning Source LLC
Chambersburg PA
CBHW071557210326
41597CB00019B/3282